Children with Literacy Difficulties

Edited by

Pat Pinsent
(Principal Lecturer in English,
The Roehampton Institute)

David Fulton Publishers

London
Published in association with the Roehampton Institute

61135

David Fulton Publishers Ltd
2 Barbon Close, Great Ormond Street, London WC1N 3JX

First published in Great Britain by
David Fulton Publishers, 1990

Note: The right of contributors to be identified as authors of their work has been asserted by them in accordance with the Copyright, Designs and Patents Act 1988.

© David Fulton Publishers 1990

British Library Cataloguing in Publication Data

Children with literacy difficulties.
1. Great Britain. Children. Literacy. Development
I. Pinsent, Pat
302.22440941

ISBN 1-85346-140-7

Typeset by Chapterhouse, Formby L37 3PX
Printed in Great Britain by BPCC Wheatons Ltd, Exeter

Children with
Literacy Difficulties

Contents

Notes on Contributors

PAT PINSENT has worked for many years at Roehampton on various INSET courses in Language and Reading, including the MA (Educational Studies). She also teaches English, including Children's Literature, to undergraduates.

SUE CARLESS and BARBARA HEARN are both support teachers, helping primary age children who have reading and writing difficulties.

ANNE BAYNE is a secondary school English teacher and co-ordinator of special needs who has a particular interest in peer tutoring.

PHILIP JONES teaches in an Infant School in south London, and also provides in-service to teachers in the areas of record-keeping, assessment and classroom management.

JEAN AUGUR is Education Officer of the British Dyslexia Association and has run a number of courses, both in England and abroad, for teachers who seek more expertise in the area of dyslexia.

HELEN KEENE is a primary school teacher currently working in a Unit for Language impaired children.

NATA GOULANDRIS formerly taught at the Dyslexia clinic at St. Bartholomew's Hospital, and is currently working as a research psychologist at the National Hospital's College of Speech Sciences and University College London. She also tutors a course on the teaching of children with specific learning difficulties.

BARBARA NOAD originally trained as an Occupational Therapist. Since qualifying as a teacher, she has worked exclusively in the field of Special Needs, including Specific Learning Disabilities.

ANN BALDWIN has worked for many years in secondary school English departments and has also run INSET courses. She is currently taking up a position of responsibility for curriculum development in a school for Gifted Children in Berkeley, California.

CELIA SNAITH was trained in Art before going into teaching as a mature student. She has taught Special Needs children in mainstream schools and now works in a Special School for children with Moderate Learning Difficulties.

ANNE WASHTELL was until recently a classroom teacher in an ILEA primary school. She is now lecturing in Language in Education at the Roehampton Institute.

Introduction

Pat Pinsent

Discussion of the subject of 'literacy' is often accompanied by a rise in the emotional temperatures of those involved. 'The young are all illiterate these days . . . It was different in my young day' is not a totally exaggerated version of such conversations. Yet evidence shows that levels of literacy in school children have in fact increased throughout this century. So too, of course, have the levels required to function effectively within a society which makes heavy demands on adult citizens if they are to play a responsible role. Filling in a form for a driving licence is a fairly trivial though significant example; what is more important is that the adult needs to possess the ability to analyse and synthesise material, whether written or spoken, in such a way as to exercise mature judgment on its worth – an ability which it is difficult to attain in the absence of a fairly high degree of literacy.

At the same time, the pressures acting against children acquiring an interest in written material are considerable, and there are those who suggest that technology is making outdated the traditional emphasis in school on reading and writing. It will soon be possible, they contend, to apply for a driving licence without filling in a form at all. The old utilitarian arguments to encourage the reluctant reader or writer may soon no longer hold, while the temptation to seek entertainment in forms more immediately accessible than books is difficult to resist.

In our society then it is particularly important to emphasise that literacy is not only the right of every individual, but also a means of enabling people to exercise their other rights (and incidentally to derive much pleasure from the process). It is vital to the attainment of autonomy. It would be too easy to say, of the kind of children we are concerned with in the articles which follow, 'Well, if they find reading and writing difficult, perhaps they needn't bother too much. They may not need it when they grow up.' People who do not reach a reasonable standard of literacy are in danger of being pawns in the hands of the literate elite. They are also likely to see themselves as less competent, less in control of their lives, than the rest of us.

Until fairly recently, a book such as this might well have been concerned only with children who have 'reading' difficulties. Perhaps there might have been a companion volume discussing children with problems in writing, particularly spelling and handwriting. Today, it is almost impossible to consider any language process in isolation, especially within the primary school curriculum. Language has sometimes been divided into four areas: speaking, listening, reading and writing, with the first and last of these being thought of as relatively active and the others as more passive. This division, while convenient, overlooks the considerable degree of activity needed in order to listen or read with comprehension and to integrate what is received into a coherent mental picture.

Any sub-dividing of the language processes runs the danger that it will minimise the interdependence of these processes. Reading and writing can scarcely be achieved without a reasonable degree of proficiency in oral language. It used to be rather facilely assumed, in spite of all the evidence to the contrary, that a child who could speak reasonably fluently would have no problems with the written language. The converse to this may well frequently be true, for a child who cannot speak adequately is highly likely to have difficulty in learning to read and write. But closer analysis of the kind of language used orally and in books reveals that much of the interaction in which pre-school children are involved is heavily dependent on the presence of the person addressed. The child faced with the demands of literacy, however, has to be able to read a written message in the absence of the person who wrote it, and to write one in the absence of the person who is going to read it. The kind of words and style used are likely to be quite different from much of what the child has experienced up to that time, for the message must be intelligible without gestures and tone of voice and everything which gives it a non-verbal context.

Learning to read and to write will therefore make heavy demands on the kind of oral language a child needs to be familiar with, and will inevitably affect the child's own language and the thought processes associated with it. Because of constraints of space, it is not possible here to give explicit attention to oral language in itself, but its close links with literacy are discussed within several of the articles, and the work of Donaldson (1978), Brown (1982), Wells (1986) and Barrs (1989, 1990) has influenced the thinking of many of the contributors.

In addition to the fact that oral language development is intrinsic to them both, the processes of learning to read and learning to write themselves cannot be regarded as separate phenomena. They develop together, are often taught together, and inevitably interact, so that someone who is behind in one is probably behind in the other.

It is perhaps particularly difficult for the teacher who is without much classroom experience to identify the children in the class who have specific problems in reading and writing, as distinct from those who are also behind their classmates in literacy but may have other reasons, physical or environmental, for their lack of progress. The first chapter of this book represents an attempt to classify some of the other factors which may inhibit success, and also gives some indication of approaches which may enable the teacher to determine the level of progress in reading and writing which has been made.

Thinking about reading, writing and oral language has developed radically within the last few years, perhaps nowhere more obviously than in the area of what is now termed 'emergent literacy'. 'Orthodoxy' on the subject of reading once demanded that parents kept out of the process of their children becoming literate, a process which did not start until they reached school age. Following the work of Clay (1975; 1982) and Clark (1976), it is now widely recognised that many children make a good start on literacy before arriving at school and that the conditions which have caused them to succeed have implications for all. Parents are now generally regarded as allies in their children's acquisition of literacy, and Sue Carless and Barbara Hearn show how the teacher may make good use of this involvement, especially by making them familiar with different ways of reading with their children. Anne Bayne presents some recent research on how other non-experts, such as older children, may also increasingly support less able readers while at the same time frequently improving their own confidence and literacy.

In order to made adequate provision for children who are finding learning difficult, it is essential that the classroom be managed in such a way as to make the process of acquiring literacy an attractive one. This means that the teacher must be aware not only of the need to organise material resources and time, but also of modes of dealing with children who do not respond so readily as the rest of the class. Philip Jones gives attention to this key aspect. Jean Augur's article focuses particularly on the dyslexic child in the classroom, and she emphasises that by becoming better teachers of children with literacy problems, we shall at the same time become better teachers of all children.

The articles by Helen Keene, Nata Goulandris and Barbara Noad give particular attention to aspects of the writing process. Keene provides a wide range of ideas which may motivate the child who is reluctant to write; her approach is grounded throughout in what has been effective in the classroom. Goulandris draws on a considerable amount of research in order to present some practical suggestions to help the children who do not 'catch' spelling in the usual way. Noad looks at perceptual motor difficulties and how these may result in the inability of children to use their bodies efficiently. This may be displayed not only in poor handwriting but also underachievement in other classroom activities. She outlines some strategies and resources relevant to this area.

Reading and writing are especially difficult to separate as discrete skills when the word processor is used. At which points are the children writing their work by using the keyboard or reading it by looking at the screen? What part does the dialogue between them as they debate what to write and how to present it play in their learning? Ann Baldwin's chapter results from her interest in the use of the computer with children of various ages and ability levels.

Children who have difficulties of a verbal nature may often have strengths in the area of spatial skills, especially art. Celia Snaith's investigations into this area have led her to believe that the ability of some of these children is too often ignored, and that it can contribute in a positive way to their literacy development.

Finally, Anne Washtell presents some fascinating observations of the way a child's learning how to write her own name involved this child, who otherwise showed every sign of being someone who would find learning to read and write difficult, in a range of 'literacy events'. Instances like these, of children making progress, despite all the obstacles which stand in their way, are those which must underlie all theory and remind the teacher of what can be achieved, sometimes against all the odds. By observing them, the teacher may learn as much as the child. In our society, children have a right to literacy; as teachers we must make ourselves aware of all the ways in which we can allow them to claim that right for themselves.

CHAPTER 1

Assessing the Problem

Pat Pinsent

Is there a problem?

The National Curriculum imposes the requirement for teachers to monitor their pupils' progress, both formally and informally, throughout their school careers. To a considerable extent, at least the informal aspect of this process is something which many teachers have been doing for many years, in their own record keeping.

Some children experience such acute difficulties in reading and writing that no teacher could have the slightest doubt that they require help. What is needed is to determine the form which that help should take, a process which will include the attempt to discover the cause of the child's problems.

In many cases, however, the situation is not so clear cut, and the teacher needs to have a perspective from which to assess the children's attainment in order to decide whether or not they have literacy problems as such, or are experiencing difficulties which result from one general factor such as health or environment. This chapter, therefore, represents an attempt to provide a broader context for children's failure to achieve a desired level in reading and writing.

It is also necessary to look briefly at approaches to the determining of relative levels of literacy ability, in the shape of some kind of measure of attainment. While the teacher, with increasing experience, is likely to be the best judge of whether a child is making the expected degree of progress and if special help is required, she may sometimes find it useful to have some independent method of assessment, such as

1

formal or informal testing, which may support her judgement, or provide more information about the specific problems of the child.

Some factors which may contribute to literacy problems

Physical factors

There is a good deal of evidence that relatively minor *hearing* defects may be of considerable significance in contributing to reading difficulties. Children with major hearing loss and an overall lack of aural acuity will normally be identified by medical tests, and will need special treatment, but the less obvious feature of inadequate auditory discrimination may be of considerable significance, as has been shown by Bryant and Bradley (1985). A child who cannot hear the difference between 'p' and 'b' or 'th' and 'f' will be unlikely to build up the kind of understanding of the relationship between sounds and how they are written which is necessary in order to go beyond the very early stages of learning to read. If a child cannot recognise that there are three sounds in the word 'pet', for instance, the possibility of spelling the word correctly without help is fairly remote. Experiences of failures of this kind are likely to create the impression in children that reading and writing are mysterious processes which require abilities that they do not have. A teacher needs to be able to recognise children who may, perhaps for fairly short periods, suffer from this problem so that she can avoid using approaches and materials which may give them a poor self image. Instead, she can concentrate on fun oral activities like nursery rhymes and jingles which build up their discriminatory abilities, while ensuring that the reading materials used hold children's interest by having a meaning relevant to the child, and, where appropriate, telling an interesting story.

The role of *visual* perception in reading might seem fairly obvious; in the extreme, a blind child cannot learn to read in the usual way. Children who have poor sight should of course be receiving treatment for this, particularly since it may hamper their ability to see words as a whole, or to develop the kind of visual imagery they need in order to acquire sight-word vocabulary. If, however, they do not readily notice the differences between 'b' and 'd', or 'p' and 'q', this is more likely to be because they do not understand the significance of orientation than as a result of poor sight as such. The kind of formal training in visual perception which concentrated on symbols rather than words or letters and was practised in some schools, is now generally disfavoured; the best way of helping children perceive and discriminate between letters and between words is within a context of meaning and the need to use these symbols in order to read or to write.

Poor manual skills, even if these merely result from immaturity, can badly affect the ability to write. The close link between reading and writing which quite rightly exists in much initial literacy teaching today means that lack of progress in one is likely to be related to failure in the other. If a child has severe problems in this area, the teacher may need to devise other ways of recording the child's ideas, for instance with a word processor.

Illness, resulting in poor attendance which impedes continuity of learning, or in impaired concentration, is likely to affect the child's progress overall, not just the literacy area. The same is true both of an *inadequate home background*, where the child may be malnourished or badly clad, and of *delayed maturation*. The particular significance of any of these factors in relation to literacy is that they may result in a child having a poor self image. This demands particular care from the teacher about the choice of material which may help the child to build up confidence.

Neurological factors (for instance epilepsy or brain damage) are rarer than those mentioned above, but like them are in most cases likely to affect all areas of a child's learning. They are also probably beyond a teacher's competence to assess. It is however worth mentioning that some theorists suggest that minimal cerebral disfunction may be related to speech and language disorders, in particular dyslexia.

Emotional factors

While depressive or psychotic illness in children is rare, it is common for them to be affected by matters concerned with relationships. Family tensions or break-up, sibling rivalry, undue parental pressure, racism or bullying at school, are all matters which may affect achievement, and it is quite possible for this to be reflected in a single area of a child's work: for instance, a parent may be over-anxious about reading because s/he also had problems at school, but less worried about number work, and may therefore by applying pressure in this area only. For some reason, even today, it is fairly acceptable to say 'I never could do Maths!' but regarded as socially demeaning to be poor at reading or writing, and this can compound a difficulty.

Teachers should not forget that they themselves and their relationship with the child may also be part of the problem!

4

Language factors

It is simplistic to describe a child's language as 'deprived'; the research of Tizard and Hughes (1984) and others has shown that the language associated with the 'working' class often provides a rich linguistic environment for a child. It is possible that a few children may have had *insufficient language interaction*, whether because they have been left alone in front of the television for long periods, because they have been left in the care of people who are not competent in English (foreign grandparents, au pairs, etc) or because they have particularly silent parents. Such aspects are not class related, but clearly any child whose language is immature for such reasons needs a good deal of interaction at school, with the teacher and with the pupils. It is quite possible that such children may not be ready to make a start on reading, but teachers should be reluctant to assume this unless they have evidence.

A related factor is the *lack of experience of story*. The research of Wells (1987) shows this to be of vital importance in children's success in reading. Children may come from homes where they do not see or handle books, and have not been read to or had stories told to them. Since most early reading material is narrative-based, it is possible that they may be unready to enjoy stories in books. It is also likely that they will lack the experience of 'book language' and find both 'story-time' and reading material alienating. They may also lack any experience of seeing adults reading or writing.

Children may speak a *non-standard variety of English*, while the books which they are given to read will be written in standard English. Most children surmount this without undue difficulty, but in some cases the vocabulary may be unfamiliar. More significant perhaps is the fact that their accent may not make use of certain sounds (for instance using 'f' for 'th' in 'thin', or 'd' for 'th' in 'the'), and this can make the relationship between the way a word is spelt and pronounced seem arbitrary to them.

In all these cases, an additional factor is that of the *teacher's expectation*. Since most teachers are likely themselves to have experienced language-rich environments, and to have provided these to their own children if they have any, there is a considerable danger that they will think of the children who lack certain kinds of language experience as less able, less ready to learn.

The child whose first language is not English naturally has particular problems in the reading and writing areas, but it is likely that the teacher will be aware of this situation. Resources to help such children are often however limited, and a teacher who has not had any special training may often find herself confronted with children who need extra help with their English. The issue is too big to be dealt with here, and it is important that teachers should not assume that such children will automatically have reading and writing difficulties. It is however worth noting that language is best learnt in use, rather than through decontextualised exercises, and most young second language learners do best when provided with extra support within the ordinary classroom rather than in a special language unit. Progress in reading is generally greatest where children are either already literate in their own language and so know what the process is all about, or have made sufficient progress in oral English to undertand the material in the books. Children sometimes manage to conceal their lack of comprehension remarkably well, and teachers should not let apparently correct answers deceive them as to the extent to which a child understands the deeper meaning of what has been said or written. It is not uncommon for a second language learner to know the meaning of all the individual words without grasping the total message.

Dyslexia

This is not the appropriate place to enter into the many controversies about dyslexia, or specific reading and language retardation. If all or most of the above factors have been ruled out, and the child is not of below average ability in general terms, it may well be that the child is dyslexic. Whether or not this diagnosis is helpful to the child and their parents is a very individual matter. Approaches which may help the child are discussed in chapter five.

Failure in reading and writing is seldom, if ever, an isolated phenomenon. It may result from more than one factor, and is likely to get worse as the child gets further behind, with the consequent effects on understanding school-work generally, on teachers' and possibly parents' expectations of the child's ability, and, probably most damaging, on the child's own self-image.

Determining the nature and extent of the problem

The teacher's own judgment is likely to be the most valid measure of whether or nor there is a literacy problem. This judgment may however need some guidance, particularly in the case of the inexperienced teacher who has not yet formed criteria as to what constitutes a good, an average or a weak reader or writer. Even the experienced teacher may sometimes need the support of what may appear to be a more 'objective' measure in order to convince colleagues of the reality of the problem. Within the framework of the National Curriculum, records of the literacy and oral language attainment of children will be kept, and in most cases these are likely to provide sufficient indication of progress or the lack of it. If further information is required, a teacher may want to use formal or informal testing techniques, which will enable her/him to acquire a sense of what can be expected at a particular level from a child, and thus to recognise those children who do not seem able to attain this standard.

Assessment of reading – informal approaches

In many circumstances, these will provide enough information and even the basis for comparison between children, without resort to any standardised tests. The *Primary Language Record* (1989) and its associated handbook, together with *Patterns of Learning* (1990), which related it explicitly to the National Curriculum, provides a straightforward means of regularly documenting observations of the child's reading, writing and oral language, together with more detailed information on some of the approaches mentioned in this chapter. The headings alert teachers to features of the child's reading, and there is also the opportunity to document the books read. This, together with the child's response to these books and attitude to reading in general, is perhaps the single most important indicator of progress or lack of progress in the field of literacy. The opportunity for self-assessment by the child should not be neglected – not explicitly by describing themselves as good or poor readers, but by keeping their own lists and comments about books read. While teachers may want to have access to these for their own records, the child's right to privacy about their responses should also be respected.

Informal assessment

The teacher creates a relaxed atmosphere, perhaps encouraging the child to choose the book which will be read. The child may preview the text with the teacher, and/or read through it silently first. A section can be practised before reading to the teacher; the text may be discussed with the teacher afterwards. During the actual reading, the teacher will be concentrating on the overall impression created, any specific strategies the child uses, and the child's responses to the text. The result of this should be that the teacher is looking at the child's reading more thoughtfully than if hearing the child read were merely a matter of noting mistakes and recording the page reached.

Running record

This is a slightly more formal process, where the teacher may note any departures that the child makes from the actual text, and also the comments which the child makes. Each error is scrutinised to see what caused the child to make it – for instance, a search for meaning or a visual cue. Self-corrections are particularly important.

Miscue

There are various methods of carrying out this process, described, for instance, in *The Primary Language Record Handbook* (1989), Southgate (1981), Arnold (1982), etc. Each teacher will probably need to devise their own preference, balancing the time spent on carrying it out against the need to gain insight into the child's reading processes. Ideally a tape recorder is used so that the child is not distracted by the teacher making notes. The child is given a piece to read which is likely to be slightly above her/his usual reading level. The piece of about 150 to 200 words, should first be read silently by the child, and may then be retold. The actual reading aloud follows, and from it, or the recording of it, the teacher codes in a consistent way, all substitutions, self-corrections, repetitions, omissions, insertions, reversals, hesitations, long pauses and refusals. These are then divided into positive and negative miscues according to the extent to which they display the child as reading for meaning. The kind of strategies used may also be divided into grapho-phonic, where the word read resembles that in the text in appearance and/or sound; syntactic, where it is grammatically appropriate; and semantic, where the meaning is accurately conveyed. The balance between the different kinds of strategies gives a good indication of the relative strengths and weaknesses of the reader, and therefore of the most appropriate kind of teaching emphasis.

Miscue is perhaps the most illuminating way of investigating the child's reading ability, but it is time consuming, and teachers may well wish to simplify the process to suit their own needs.

Informal reading inventory

The teacher makes a collection of passages, graded for difficulty. Employing texts where some indication is given as to level of difficulty may be appropriate here, or use can be made of readability formulae (see Harrison, 1980), preferably derived by using a computer. The child either starts with the first passage, or at a point which the teacher thinks appropriate. The teacher may simply make a count of the number of errors in order to determine if the child is reading at independent level (99–100% word recognition), instructional level (95–98%) or frustration level (below 95%). The difference between these levels is marked by the difference between fluent reading with excellent comprehension, and disjointed reading, one word at a time, with patchy understanding. This technique is particularly useful to gauge the reading ability of a new arrival to the class.

Cloze

The deletion of words in a prepared passage is a very flexible device, which is used in a number of standardised tests and may also be employed to test the readability of a passage. Its use as a teaching method, preferably in group work, should not be neglected.

In relation to informal testing, cloze may be used in various ways, as suggested by Rye (1982). Random deletions (from one in five to one in ten, avoiding proper names or any information which reading out of context could not be expected to supply) can provide a measure of the relative ability of various children, though the degree of familiarity or interest in the subject matter needs to be taken into account here. The way a child replaces the deletions gives an indication of her/his reading ability. If cloze is used in an informal way, there is no need to demand the exact words of the passage, but this may be necessary if comparisons are to be made between children, as an element of subjectivity comes in when synonyms are allowed.

As an alternative to random deletions, deletion of function words (such as 'to', 'was', 'the') can also be informative about any problems concerned with syntax. Cloze can also be used to assess comprehension of a subject, if key words associated with the subject are deleted. A good deal of insight into the child's reading process can be gained if some of the substitutions are examined – are they syntactically appropriate? Do they indicate a use of post context as well as prior context?

Some theorists object to the use of cloze because it is presenting children with a distorted text. Care should therefore be taken that its use is not excessive.

Standardised reading tests

The use of tests which have been standardised by submitting them to a number of children is of limited utility, particularly if they have been devised many years ago, or consist merely of a list of words which increase in difficulty but have no context. They may nevertheless be valuable if any comparisons need to be made, for instance between schools, classes, groups, individual children, or even the same child at two different times. They can be useful to test the efficacy of a research project when pupils have, for instance, been subjected to different approaches to the teaching of reading. They are often used as part of a screening process, in order to identify children who have problems, and may often be required in order to set in progress the provision of extra help for such children. These tests should not, however, be thought of as being totally objective. Different tests, and even different forms of the same test, will give totally different results in terms of reading age, as shown by Laycock (1989). Useful criteria for choosing which tests to use can be found in Vincent *et al.* (1983) and Pumfrey (1985), but new tests are frequently devised, and others are updated. Many modern tests avoid the questionable concept of reading age replacing it by banded scores which enable the teacher to estimate relative positions of children without the rigidity of a reading age.

A few examples of useful tests are given here, but these should not be taken as in any way limiting. With these and all tests, careful attention should be given to the instruction booklets, which indicate how the tests should be used and how they have been standardised.

(1) *Group Literacy Assessment* (1982). This consists of a single sheet with two passages on it; one provides misspelled items in a short story and the other is a reasonably entertaining cloze test. Vincent *et al.* (1983) describe it as a 'reading-dependent test of spelling'. Its interest level is designed for children aged 10 to 12, and it gives reading ages which range from 7 to 14. It is quick and easy to use, and often enjoyed by children.

(2) *The New Macmillan Reading Analysis* (1985). This consists of three series each of six graded passages. It is administered individually, the process taking about fifteen minutes. As well as

assessing reading progress in the early Junior years, it can be used for diagnosis with children of any age who may be experiencing reading problems. A count is made of the number of oral reading errors, and testing stops if a child makes sixteen errors on any one of the first five passages of the group of six. At the end of each passage there are oral questions about its meaning. This leads to a score which may be related to an age equivalent band: for instance a score of 62 on Form A is equivalent to an age range from 8.9 to 9.10. More detailed analysis of types of error – substitution, insertion, omission, reversal, refusal, hesitation, repetition and self-correction – enables the tester to observe reading behaviour, as in miscue analysis, to diagnose strengths and weaknesses, and thus to put into action appropriate remedial strategies. The passages are varied and generally fairly interesting, though, as the compilers admit, 'The stylistic imperfections of the sixth passage demonstrate the limits to which oral reading assessment can realistically be applied.'

(3)   *Macmillan Effective Reading Tests* (1987/9). This series of group reading tests (hence more economical on time than (2)) covers six levels from infant to secondary, providing detailed information about children's progress. In particular, these tests involve comprehension of longer narrative texts. Each level includes an attractive story booklet which children are likely to enjoy reading for its own sake, and the questions range from very easy ones at level 0 to quite sophisticated ones which demand the ability to scan text for the more able reader. With a reasonable range of these tests and a judicious choice of level (all of which overlap), a teacher would have the opportunity to complete the process without drawing too much attention to the less able reader. There is also some opportunity for diagnosis of types of reading difficulty, as the questions are arranged to assess different kinds of abilities, such as following the thread of sentences and paragraphs, interpreting diagrams and pictures, and predicting what is going to happen. The results are given with a standardised score conversion table, dispensing with the concept of reading age.

Diagnostic tests

As indicated in the descriptions of the tests above, standardised tests can often be used to diagnose the type of reading difficulty a child may have. Some tests, however, concentrate entirely on this aspect.

(1) *Concepts about Print.* This forms part of Marie Clay's *Early Detection of Reading Difficulties* (Heinemann, 1972/9) but many teachers have found the use of one or both of the specially printed books, *Sand* and *Stones*, on their own, helpful in assessing the progress of children in the early stages of learning to read. The booklets cover the conventions of print, the language of reading instruction, and knowledge about punctuation; they include words and letters in the wrong order or upside down, and can be quite entertaining to use. The 1979 edition gives full details of Clay's Reading Recovery Programme.

(2) *Assessing Reading Difficulties* (1980). This test devised by Bradley concentrates on auditory discrimination in young children, though it may be adapted for older pupils with reading difficulty. It is quick and easy to administer.

(3) *Macmillan Diagnostic Reading Pack* (1980). This is intended for children with reading ages from six to nine, and deals with a wide range of 'reading skills' from letter recognition to blends, digraphs, and more generalised reading strategies. While its approach may seem to depend on a rather mechanistic view of reading, use of it could certainly alert teachers to aspects of a child's reading which they had not observed.

(4) *The Bangor Dyslexia Test* (1982). This is not a reading test as such, consisting rather of tests of left/right differentiation, repeating polysyllabic words, mental arithmetic, reversals of sequences, and investigation of familial incidence of difficulty with written language. It is intended to be used as part of a wider assessment in conjunction with observation of the child's reading and writing.

Assessing writing

It is less easy to find any standardised criteria by which to assess children's writing than it is for reading. The National Writing Project's *Responding to and Assessing Writing* (1989) gives more attention to response than to assessment, and while educationally this is undoubtedly the priority, there are times when a teacher may need to have some idea of how a child's writing compares with that of others of a similar age. Examples of children's work for this kind of comparison can be found in a variety of sources, such as the wide range of booklets produced by the National Writing Project itself and the specimens published by The Assessment of Performance Unit (APU). The appendix to *English from 5 to 11* (the first part of the Cox Report) and the examples given by Temple, Nathan and Burris (1988) are also useful. *Assessing Language Development*, by Wilkinson, Barnsley, Hanna and Swann (1980) presents the results of a study of the writing of children aged seven, ten and thirteen on several different kinds of topics, and analyses them in terms of cognitive development, moral development, affective development and style. The criteria established are too detailed to be used in any everyday way in the classroom, but can be very informative if applied to the work of an individual who needs closer study.

Associated with the *Concepts about Print* test mentioned above, Clay (1975, 1979) puts forward writing test procedures for children in the early stages of schooling. These consist of the evaluation of writing samples in terms of 'Language Level', 'Message Quality' and 'Directional Principles', a test of writing vocabulary by asking the child to write down all the words she/he knows in ten minutes, and dictation tests which give credit for every sound written correctly.

An alternative approach is to consider some of the factors which apply to writing and examine the child's progress under these headings. An example of this follows. Note that this begins with technical aspects, since these are easier to measure. It does not imply that these are the most important. In some instances the distinction is drawn between dialect uses and standard English. This is not to imply that children should be discouraged from using their own dialect, but rather that they should be led to an awareness that in writing, certainly as they reach the stage when public examinations will be taken, standard English is often expected where dialect might be acceptable in speech.

Some factors to consider when assessing writing

- *Handwriting.* Is it legible? Flowing? In a style appropriate to the child's development?
- *Spelling.* How many mistakes are there? Are the mistakes phonologically correct, phonologically incorrect but near to visual accuracy, or neither?
- *Punctuation.* Are the mistakes omissions, substitutions or additions? Do they relate to full-stops and capital letters, quotation marks, commas, colons, semi-colons? (Note that the

use of commas etc. causes many problems to adults as well as children!)

- *Grammar*. This term applies to syntax, which is concerned with the order of the words, and morphology (or accidence) which is concerned with the form of words, their endings and how they change (for instance, pronouns, verb endings for past, present, singular, plural, etc.). In both cases, the distinction needs to be drawn between forms which are acceptable in writing, those which are acceptable in speech but not normally in writing except where speech is being reported (such as contractions like 'I shan't'), those which are acceptable in dialect but not in standard English (e.g. 'We was there', 'I done it'), and those which are unacceptable in any form of English (such as 'I am so much loving your country beautiful'). When looking at the work of young children, attention needs to be given to the appearance of transitional forms which are not part of any English dialect but which may be part of their development of a system of rules (such as 'I hitted him'). These are generally outgrown without difficulty.

- *Vocabulary*. Are the words which are chosen appropriate, interesting, repetitive, dialect or standard English, etc.?

- *Audience*. What kind of audience does the writer seem to have been aiming for: teacher/parent/self/other children in the class/other children in the school/unknown adults, etc.? Does the writer seem to understand how much knowledge this audience has, and to give any necessary explanations?

- *Function*. What is the writing for? Is it intended to instruct, to persuade, work out the writer's own ideas, remind about something that should not be forgotten, enjoy language for its own sake, tell a story, etc? Does it perform its function well? If it is a story, is it consistent? Do the characters seem real (if this is what is wanted)? Does the plot hold together? If fantasy is present, does it seem convincing?

- *Shape*. Has the piece a beginning, middle and end, if this is needed? If it is a poem, does it seem to be in the right form? Does it, and should it, rhyme? Is the piece of writing long enough, or even too long, for its purpose? Does it seem the kind of length you would have expected from your knowledge of the writer?

- *Overall factors*. Does it convey feeling, if this seems needed? Do you like it? Is the writer satisfied with it? Should it be redrafted? Is it worth making into a book? Should it reach a wider audience?

14

If so, what kind of audience, and how should it be presented?

These questions are by no means limiting, but give some idea of factors which are relevant to judging children's writing, bearing in mind the age and ability of the children concerned. Teachers need to evolve their own framework of criteria.

Conclusion

Although the process of assessment, whether formal or informal, can seem one of the more time consuming and less interesting aspects of a teacher's work, it is essential, particularly when we are dealing with children who have literacy problems. A knowledge of the levels of achievement of children of a wide range of ability must form the basis for any evaluation of the work of children who seem to fall behind the normal levels in any part of their school work. The teacher also needs to be careful about the kind of response given to reading or writing, so that whatever the level of achievement, the child is not left with a feeling of failure.

References

Ames, T. (1980). *The Macmillan Diagnostic Reading Pack*. London: Macmillan.
Bradley, L. (1980). *Assessing Reading Difficulties*. London: Macmillan.
Clay, M.M. (1979). *The Early Detection of Reading Difficulties*. London: Heinemann.
Clay, M.M. (1972). *Sand*. London: Heinemann.
Miles, T.R. (1982). *The Bangor Dyslexia Test*. Wisbech: LDA.
Spooncer, F.A. (1981). *Group Literacy Assessment*. London: Hodder & Stoughton.
Vincent, D. and De La Mare, M. (1986, 1989). *Effective Reading Tests*. London: Macmillan.
Vincent, D. and De La Mare, M. (1985). *New Macmillan Reading Analysis*. London: Macmillan.

CHAPTER 2

Parental Involvement with Reading

Sue Carless and Barbara Hearn

> Parents, renouncing their bit part as peripheral irritants in the education system, have moved centre stage. (Topping, 1986)

Since these words were written, parents have moved even more to the forefront of education, with recent Education Acts giving greater access to the curriculum and the running of the schools. Parents are now directly involved in many areas of school life, and one of the main aspects of this has been the involvement of parents in helping their children learn to read. The initial parental involvement projects were set up in areas where there was concern about children's reading progress and all the children in a class or school were included. The success of these projects encouraged the setting up of similar schemes in a wide variety of schools, ranging from those who had many children with reading problems to those who had few. Children with severe reading difficulties were, of course, included in the projects. However, such projects are not always productive for these children; both they and their parents often need more precise guidelines and more frequent support than is possible in a whole class scheme. For this reason specific methods have been incorporated into projects which have been set up for the parents of children with reading difficulties.

Before we consider the different approaches that teachers might show parents it is worth considering how such an explosion of interest in parental involvement in reading has come about. It seems to us that two separate strands have merged to combine over the last twenty years; on the one hand, parental involvement in daily school life and

16

on the other hand, the idea of the parent as educator as well as rearer.

Before the 1960s, parents were not often assigned an active role in their child's education. The survey of J. W. B. Douglas (1964) began a change in attitude by the teaching profession; he found, from the factors he considered, that parental interest was the most powerful indicator of academic success at ages eight and eleven. Soon after came the Plowden Report (1967) which was the first official recognition of the important role parents have in the education of their children. The Plowden Report recommended that parents be kept informed both about their child specifically and about school policy in general. The report highlighted a problem of poor communication between home and school.

> Teachers are linked to parents by the children for whom they are both responsible. The triangle should be completed and a more direct relationship established between teachers and parents. They should be partners in more than name; their responsibility becomes joint instead of several.
>
> (Vol. 1, p. 30)

Many of the changes in home/school relationships have developed in response to Plowden initiatives. The Home and School Council was set up in 1967 to bring parents and teachers closer together. Plowden's views were endorsed in further official reports such as the Taylor Report (1977) on school management whose recommendations included the proposal that parents, elected by other parents, should make up a quarter of a school's governing body and that there should be increased information for parents both about their child and the school. The Warnock Report (1978) on special educational needs stressed reciprocal relationships between parents and professionals.

> Parents can be effective partners only if professionals take notice of what they say . . . and treat their contribution as intrinsically important

These comments seem particularly relevant to home-reading projects, which involve children with literacy problems, as, inherent in such schemes, should be the willingness of teachers to listen to parents' comments and use them to the child's advantage.

Therefore since 1967 there has been much official endorsement of the parental role in education. There have also been specific studies where parental involvement has been seen in action rather than in theory. Originally there was a tendency to regard middle class parents as having high aspirations for their children, and few problems were anticipated when involving them in their child's education. Working class parents, however, were viewed as less ambitious, apathetic and both afraid and unable to help. K. Roberts (1980) suggests that such stereotypes can be misleading. Working class ambitions were being underestimated and a too harmonious picture of middle class home-school relationships was presented. Young and McGeeney (1968) set up a parental involvement project in a working class area and found a 'passionate but impotent interest' and an 'untapped source of strength to the school'. Newson and Newson (1977) found in a survey of seven year olds that many working class parents helped their children with their reading whether asked to or not by the school. Tizard and Hewison (1980) reported on Hewison's investigations into factors influencing the reading attainment of seven and eight year old working class children in Dagenham. She found the most significant factor was whether or not the parents heard their child read regularly. Since that time there has been a nationwide growth in parental involvement in schools and in reading in particular.

Given the fact that a head or teacher believes in parental involvement in school, we feel that s/he must also accept the parent's role as educator in order to enter fully into a successful partnership with parents in the teaching of reading. It is no good believing that teachers teach and parents rear. During this century the non-professional educator has faded into the background with compulsory state education and the school acting *in loco parentis*. However, since the late sixties there has been a proliferation of books on the parent as teacher.

Some of the early books committed parents to giving up a great deal of time; one of these was the well known work by Glen Doman (1965) who follows a structured regime using flash cards to teach very young children to learn all manner of things. More recently there have been a number of more practical, lively books on how parents can encourage reading. Dorothy Butler (1980) believes that the love of reading begins at birth and no time is too soon for a parent to begin sharing books with his/her baby. Her book is both inspiring and soundly practical. Margaret Meek (1982) is a fierce protagonist of the parent as 'the child's natural teacher.' She gives sound advice to the parent and says that '. . . there is nothing about reading that parents cannot know or understand.' Recent studies of parents talking with their children at home point towards mothers from all backgrounds teaching a great deal to their children through everyday conversation. Both Tizard and Hughes (1984) and Wells (1987) view the home as a 'powerful learning environment.' Therefore there has been a movement, in both research and books for parents, towards accepting the worth of parents as educators.

Some home-reading projects

The two strands, parental involvement in daily school life and the role of parent as educator, have merged in a number of well documented and publicized home-reading projects. Perhaps the best known is the Haringey Project (1980), set up as a result of Hewison's Dagenham research, in a multi-ethnic working class area where there had been little parental involvement previously. This was a project in which parents were asked to hear their children read two or three times a week. The parents were helped in the initial stages and throughout the project by researchers who visited them at home. The results were exceptionally good in both motivation and reading attainment, irrespective of social class or ethnic background. Many similar projects were set up as a result of Haringey's success.

In 1979 a pilot home-reading scheme was set up in Hackney, in six junior schools. Its success led to the formation of PACT (Parents and Teachers and Children) which gives advice and support to schools wanting to involve parents. Although researchers did not set rigorous assessment procedures, Griffiths and Hamilton (1984) report good results in all aspects of reading and a better relationship between parents and teachers.

A third influential project was the Belfield Reading Project in Rochdale (1978), set up in a predominantly white working class area with poor housing and high unemployment. In spite of this apparently unpromising situation, Hannon and Jackson (1987) state in their final report that they found excellent take-up, even when parents were asked to continue helping their children for three years. They found children's attitude to books and reading much improved, as were teachers' relationships with parents. The teachers felt that as a result of the project, which involved home visiting, they gained insight into home learning. The parents too were very positive, enjoying assisting their children's progress. However, the final report is interesting in that the parental involvement did not inevitably produce greatly increased reading scores. It therefore appears that, if reading scores alone are indicators of the success of parental involvement, then such schemes may not produce the desired result. This should not devalue the positive gains in attitude and interest.

A common feature of these schemes is the maintenance of home/school liaison throughout the project. Both the Haringey and the Belfield projects involved regular home visiting and this aspect is thought to be particularly valuable in keeping up the momentum. It is interesting to consider why the Haringey project appears to be more successful than the Belfield project. In the final report Hannon and Jackson (1987) suggest that, as theirs is a community school, there were already good relationships with parents, whereas there was no history of parents helping their children read in the Haringey schools. Hannon and Jackson also wonder whether the higher level of home-visiting in Haringey was a significant factor, particularly as many of the Haringey parents did not have English as a first language and therefore felt unable to help before this project.

Advantages and difficulties

Home/school reading schemes have been shown to have many advantages. In an ideal situation a parent has the time to give the child much needed practice and support with immediate feedback, praise and reward. A real dialogue between parent and teacher can develop, covering all aspects of the child's progress, with mutual respect and understanding. A well organised scheme may lead to a more purposeful involvement by the parent and hopefully enhance the child's enjoyment of literature.

When working with children who have reading and writing difficulties it is important to consider a wide range of strategies. A useful one may be the involvement of their parents. Children with literacy difficulties almost invariably find little enjoyment in books: sensitive help from their parents could well rekindle this interest, which is vital to sustain these children through their efforts in learning to read. Unfortunately, emotional problems often accompany reading failure and, whilst children need their parents' support at this particularly difficult time, this is not always easily accomplished, for a variety of reasons.

When a child has experienced failure in reading, the class or support teacher can appear to the parent as the expert and thus a genuine sharing of information can be that much more difficult. Parents may feel responsible for their child's failure and, although anxious to help, may feel impotent. There is surely a case for supporting the parent, before we can ask the parent to support the child. It is important to remember that parents often have not only fears for their child's future but also guilt at their child's inability to learn in the same way as other children. Young and Tyre (1985a) suggest that parents should be reassured that they have succeeded in teaching their child many skills already, and helping with her/his reading is only an extension of this role.

Wendy Bloom (1987) points out that parents often criticise the school in order to find someone to blame for their child's failure. She suggests that

> parents of these children need extra encouragement, support and praise for their efforts because it is probable that they harbour deep feelings of guilt and failure in themselves.

Therefore, at first the parent may need very structured guidelines of simple activities for helping the child, in an unthreatening way, so that success is ensured; for instance reading stories to the child or playing games together. In this way the parents' anxieties can be channelled into positive activity and frustration will be lessened.

However we feel that it is important to accept that there are parents who cannot help their child, perhaps because of family circumstances or the personality of the child. As busy parents ourselves, we understand the difficulties of finding an uninterrupted time that is acceptable to both parent and child. We understand too that the intense relationship experienced between parent and child can sometimes militate against the relaxed atmosphere that a less involved teacher can achieve. Although a parent may not be able to give direct help, the parent's interest must be valued. In practice we have found very few parents who are totally lacking in interest. Their interest can be supportive in itself, particularly if we as teachers can guide the parents to praise the child's efforts. This encouragement from parents must surely lead to positive feedback for the child, in that the child will be experiencing, perhaps for the first time, mutual interest and support from both home and school. It is surely very important too, in this sensitive area of education, to listen to parents and value their opinions and knowledge of their child. This sharing of knowledge between parent and teacher will almost certainly benefit the child.

Failure in school can lead to many reactions from children, including withdrawal, disruptive or aggressive behaviour, diversionary tactics or playing teacher off against parent. A solid stand by parents and teachers can to some extent counteract or minimise these behaviours. Therefore, although teachers must accept that involving parents of children with reading difficulties is not plain sailing, parents should at the very least be kept informed and urged to encourage their child, if only in word rather than deed. We feel that, where feasible, a parent's help with reading or games on a regular basis can be very supportive and this may well reap rewards in improved motivation which can lead to greater success in reading. Many different parental involvement schemes have been documented. (See Topping and Wolfendale, 1985, for a comprehensive selection.) There is no one correct method, but in the following pages we show a range of strategies that parents can use to help their children.

Listening to children read

This is the time-honoured method of involving parents with their child's reading. It is an approach with which many parents feel most at home. However, it is not without its difficulties. Unless there is frequent praise, emphasis may be given to the child's errors and it can become a negative activity. Parents sometimes have misconceptions about learning to read. They may feel that accuracy is all-important and a guess, however well informed, is undesirable; thus predictions using contextual cues may not be encouraged. We have met parents who feel that reading should be difficult and so the child is not learning if s/he reads a book with ease. Therefore, if we ask parents to hear their child read, it is important to stress a more positive approach and to model good practice for parents. This can be reinforced by providing a simple, lively booklet with ideas to help overcome difficulties and, where time permits, by liaising frequently with the parents.

Pause, prompt and praise

A more structured approach to listening to children read has been evolved in the Pause, Prompt and Praise method (Glynn, 1985). This originated in New Zealand and was based on the work of Marie Clay, which emphasised the importance of self-correction strategies and the integration of the different cueing systems in reading. This approach encourages children to develop independent strategies for reading unknown words. The parent is taught to pause for at least five seconds at a miscue or hesitation. This allows time for self-correction. If this does not occur then the parent gives one of three prompts – semantic, visual or contextual. If the child does not respond after two prompts then the parent tells the child the word. Praise is given throughout, not only for correct responses but also for good attempts that may not be quite right. (See Figure 2.1 for a flow chart giving details of the method.) This is a useful strategy, giving clear guidelines, that parents can learn to help their child who is struggling with reading. However, it is important that the reading material provided is at a level at which the child will be meeting some unknown words but can read enough of the

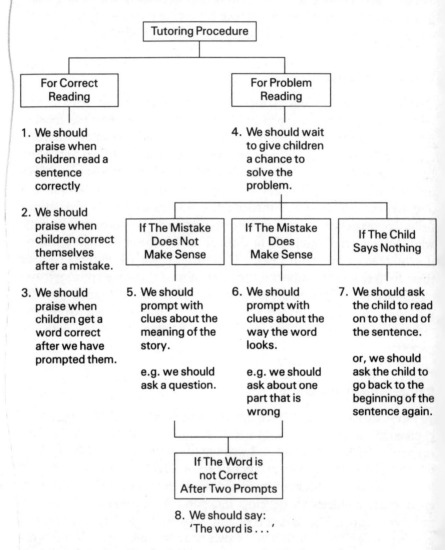

Fig 2.1 Instruction sheet for 'pause, prompt and praise' procedures.

(Reproduced with permission of Positive Products, Cheltenham)

text to make good predictions. We therefore feel that this approach. although useful, may be less suited to the beginner reader. It may well be that a form of paired reading is more appropriate for the non-starter.

Paired reading

Whilst the simple process of listening to a child read can reap rewards, a totally new approach, after what is sometimes years of failure, may be more productive. Paired reading therefore should be considered when involving parents of children with reading difficulties.

Roger Morgan first introduced this technique in 1976 and from this, many paired reading schemes, both with parents and peer tutors, have evolved. The method is clearly set out in Morgan (1986). The child is allowed a free choice of any book regardless of difficulty. There are two phases in paired reading. In phase one the parent and child read simultaneously at the child's pace, pointing to the words if necessary. It is important that neither child nor parent lags behind in the reading and that they attempt each word together. If the child is unable to read a word, or miscues, the parent points to the word again and parent and child repeat the word together before continuing. In the second phase the child signals to the parent that s/he will try reading alone, which s/he continues to do until s/he hesitates or makes a mistake. The parent then points to the mistake and asks the child to have another attempt. If, after four seconds s/he can't provide the correct word, the parent supplies the word and the parent and child read it together and immediately revert to simultaneous reading as in phase one until the child signals again. An important part of the technique is the use of praise which is built in at all levels and ensures that the child does not experience failure – vital for those children who have had years of failure with other methods. The two phases are flexible in that in the early stages or with a difficult book a child may rarely signal to read alone.

Keith Topping has done a lot of work on paired learning and has produced a video and paired reading pack (1988) which teachers would find very useful. Topping suggests many advantages in paired reading; it is easy and flexible to use, with the child taking control of the material read and the method of reading; it is a positive method with frequent praise and with failure almost totally eliminated; it models correct intonation and pronunciation and maintains the flow, so assisting comprehension; it gives practice with a much wider variety of reading matter than is possible when the child reads independently; finally, by giving the child a free choice of reading matter, it fosters the enjoyment and interest which is so vital to reading progress.

A number of successful paired reading schemes are reported in Topping and Wolfendale (1985) and improvements in fluency and particularly comprehension are noted. Other gains have been found in increased enjoyment and motivation. Whilst we feel that this is a most useful technique, we have found in practice that some parents do not take readily to it and prefer a more traditional approach. Maybe the problem lies with us, since, as support teachers, we do not always have as much time as we would like to train the parents with the children. This training and subsequent follow-up sessions would seem to be vital in maintaining a successsful paired reading scheme. We have found this is especially important with parents of children with reading difficulties.

There are a number of variations on paired reading that are worthy of consideration.

1. Five stage reading

Young and Tyre (1983) document a more structured version of paired reading. Their project did not involve liaison with schools, but parents were supported, at home, by a teacher researcher who helped the parents give daily individual tuition for thirty minutes a day over one year; the children also attended three holiday schools of a week each. The daily half-hour's tuition included a form of paired reading using books 'which respected the maturity of interest of the pupil but which were about two years below their tested levels of reading ability.' Young and Tyre suggest that the combination of paired reading and the security of reading simple material promote a greater chance of success. The parents and children also worked on word games based on their reading, spelling patterns, codes and nonsense rhyme activities. Not surprisingly with such input from the parents, the results were extremely good. Home visits were made every two weeks, but it is interesting to note that Young and Tyre (1985a) suggest that weekly support would have been better because of the demands that were being made on parents.

The paired reading was carried out in five stages:

(1) Parent and child discuss the reading material.
(2) The parent reads the passage to the child (for three minutes), pointing to the print.

(3) Parent and child read the same passage together.
(4) Parent and child read the same passage again but this time the parent stops occasionally for the child to read alone.
(5) The child reads the same passage alone. (Parent supplying any unknown words.)

This appears a very long winded approach but we have found it successful with children who have failed for many years. The repetition, which might to an adult appear boring, can be very supportive. Tony Martin (1989) used this method successfully in a middle school with children who had suffered years of failure.

2. Prepared reading

When a child is becoming more confident, it is possible to adapt the above method and use only some of the stages. Alternatively, the adult can read the passage to the child, missing out predictable words for the child to read, and then the child can attempt to read the passage independently. This ensures the child is fully involved in the first reading and therefore gives a form of preparation for the later independent reading.

Young and Tyre (1985a) suggest that for children with reading ages above eight years 'Prepared Reading' might be more suitable. The parent and child discuss the passage together, the parent then reads the passage to the child, the child reads the passage silently asking for help where necessary and then the child reads the passage alone. This can be taken a stage further when the child is gaining confidence; parent and child can read silently together and then discuss the story.

3. Shared reading

Greening and Spenceley (1987) describes a simplified version of paired reading. It is basically the first phase of paired reading, when parent and child read simultaneously, and is most useful as a modelling technique for inexperienced readers. It is different from paired reading in that the parent does not correct the child's errors and the parent reads on even if the child can only join in with a few words. Greening and Spenceley suggest that it is 'a transitional stage between hearing a story read and becoming a fluent, independent reader.' It is much simpler for a teacher to organise than paired reading but some parents of failed readers may feel that this method is not really extending their child's competence. On the other hand it can be an unthreatening way to help a child. Therefore, like the other methods we have discussed, it is worth considering.

Reading to the child

Because parents of failed readers feel that they must do something positive, they are sometimes unable to see the benefits of reading to their child. As well as being an excellent model, giving a child an experience of book language, reading to a child can foster the imagination and also keep alive an interest in literature. We find that parents are much more willing to read to their child if it is explained to them that, although the child is behind with reading, s/he should not be denied the experience of books at his/her cognitive level.

There are some books on the market designed specifically for the parent and child to take turns in reading. One example is the Ladybird *Puddle Lane* reading programme by Sheila McCullagh. At the simplest level the parent reads the full story and the child then reads a simplified version which is by the side of the parent's version, on the adjacent page. In the later books the text is continuous with no simplified repetition of the story, but the left hand page for the parent to read is a full text and the right hand page for the child is a simpler and shorter text. This is an interesting idea but we feel it gives the child an unnatural view of what reading is all about. However, a similar idea can be used with any reading book, whereby the parent reads a page and the child reads the next page. Parents often feel that this is cheating so this has to be explained and justfied to them. We have found this a useful strategy because, not only does it provide a good model, it also takes the strain of reading aloud away from the child, and makes the story move more quickly, thus aiding comprehension.

Games

Children enjoy playing games and do not regard it as work. Therefore, games are useful for involving parents. We have not found many published games that we would want to use at home, mainly because they do not reinforce exactly the aspect of reading we have been working on. However, it is possible to make simple games both with and for the children. Often a game that will prove most successful has been devised or adapted for a particular child. Parents could also be encouraged to play simple games with the text the child is reading, for example – I spy a word beginning with 'gr' or a word rhyming with 'book'. Young and Tyre (1985b) have some useful suggestions for this type of game in their book for parents.

Conclusion and summary

Over the last few years parental involvement in reading has grown until it has become an accepted mode of operation in the majority of schools. A child with reading and writing difficulties is no longer just seen by the remedial teacher twice a week; input from parents is frequently encouraged. As we have discussed earlier, this can be extremely valuable but we would still reiterate our reservations. Tread carefully! There may be some parents who, despite good intentions, find they are unable to help. This often occurs as adolescence approaches and the child seeks more independence.

In this case peer tutoring is well worth consideration and this is thoroughly documented in the following chapter.

Parents who want to help may need much extra support and encouragement. This could well be in the form of informal meetings at school, but the experience of some home-reading projects should also be considered. Home-visiting was found to be particularly fruitful in maintaining momentum, and it may be that this form of contact, although time-consuming, would be particularly valuable for parents of children with reading difficulties, where there will almost certainly be many concerns that the parents will want to discuss with the teacher. With this kind of support from the school, parental help can indeed be a valuable asset to both child and teacher.

Suggested further reading for teachers

Bloom, W. (1987). *Partnership with Parents in Reading*, London: Hodder & Stoughton.
Branston, P., Provis, M. (1986). *Children and Parents enjoying Reading*. London: Hodder & Stoughton.
Davis, C. and Stubbs, R. (1988). *Shared Reading in Practice*, Milton Keynes: Open University.
Morgan, R. (1986). *Helping Children Read*, London: Methuen.
Topping, K. and Wolfendale, S. (1985). *Parental Involvement in Children's Reading*. London: Croom Helm.
Topping, K. (1988). *Paired Reading Training* pack (Third Edition). Huddersfield: Kirklees Psychological Service.
Young, P. and Tyre, C. (1983). *Dyslexia or Illiteracy?* Milton Keynes: Open University.

Pause, Prompt and Praise, Video and Professional Handbook available from Positive Products, PO Box 45, Cheltenham, Glos.

Suggested reading list for parents

Butler, D. (1980) *Babies Need Books*. Harmondsworth: Penguin.
Butler, D. (1986). *Five to Eight*. London: Bodley Head.
Butler, D. and Clay, M. (1982). *Reading Begins at Home*. London: Heinemann.
Griffiths, A. and Hamilton, D. (1987) *Learning at Home*. London: Methuen.
Meek, M. (1982) *Learning to Read*. London: Methuen.
O'Keeffe, R. and Salt, J. (1988) *Parents' Guide to Your Child's Reading and Writing*. London: Octopus.
Root, B. (1988). *Help Your Child to Read*. London: Usborne.
Trelease, J. (1984). *The Read-Aloud Handbook*. Harmondsworth: Penguin.
Young, P. and Tyre, C. (1985). *Teach Your Child to Read*. London: Collins.

CHAPTER 3

Peer Tutoring

Anne Bayne

Many years of teaching English to mixed-ability classes in a comprehensive school led me to contemplate ways of helping those children who arrived in my lessons unable to read at a level that would enable them to cope with the curriculum. It was difficult enough for them in English lessons where at least my own understanding about the readability of texts and the development of oral language, reading and writing, enabled me to give some guidance and help. I often however wondered how they fared in subjects like Science and Geography.

It was not until my concern and curiosity took me into the field of Special Needs that, as a Support teacher, I discovered exactly what did happen in those subjects. It was this that led me to investigate ways in which these pupils could be helped. The problem was there and it might occur at all stages from the bottom juniors to the top of the secondary school. Some children were failing at all levels. It was not just a matter of teacher time, though this was short enough; it was the difficulty of overcoming the lack of self-esteem and general non-interest caused by years of failure. 'I'm thick, Miss,' was a frequent cry.

Peer tutoring seemed an obvious answer, and I wondered why I had not thought of it before. I had used the method informally within the classroom as part of my normal teaching techniques, but I never considered the implications for the curriculum of extending and formalising its use.

What is peer tutoring?

> 'Qui docet discet.' (He who teaches others, teaches himself.)
> Comenius

Peer tutoring, cross-age tutoring, pupil tutoring: these are all terms used to describe one of the oldest forms of instruction known in human history. This form of co-operative learning, the pairing of one student with another to help in the mastery of a skill, has been used throughout time. It is a very versatile approach, involving sometimes the use of students of the same age but who have reached a different stage of learning, sometimes older students to tutor younger or adults to tutor students. There are accounts of very young children being used to help their friends and of university students helping in schools; of parents acting as reading assistants and of school children tutoring junior classes.

As early as the first century A.D. Quintilian described situations where older children were tutoring younger children. This co-operative learning continued throughout history, used in many different ways. For the purposes of this work, the act of this co-operative learning will be referred to as 'peer tutoring', although for the research older students were used to tutor younger students. 'Peer' is defined as someone 'belonging to the same group in society when membership is defined by status. In this case the status is that of not being professional.' (Goodlad and Hirst, 1989).

In many ways, in an informal manner, tutoring has been used to hand on expertise. Eleven year old boys are the first to train their younger friends in the art of cricket in the nets; post-graduate students are used as demonstrators to first year medical students when they are first dissecting the body; sixth form students organise and produce plays of the junior drama club. Less informally, the whole system developed from passing on information about the new G.C.S.E., the 'cascade system', is a form of tutoring. Schemes have been described throughout the centuries; schemes developed for teachers to pass on expertise for the benefit both of the tutor and the tutee, though most schemes emphasise the benefit to the tutee. However, it was Comenius who said, some three centuries ago:

> The saying 'he who teaches others, teaches himself', is very true, not only because constant repetition impresses a fact indelibly on the mind, but because the process of teaching itself gives a deeper insight into the subject taught . . .

(John Amos Comenius, quoted in *The Great Didactic*, Wright, 1960, p. 354).

Most teachers would agree that this advice is indeed true, and most would agree that they themselves have learned something new in every lesson taught. A new slant, a fresh perspective, are excitements experienced by every teacher.

Tutoring can, therefore, be seen to be of advantage to the tutee, in that there is the extra input given in individual teaching. It is also of advantage to the tutor, in that the 'teacher' is learning by teaching. Other advantages have also been described. Learning may occur in a way that is an alternative to competition. This helping of others gives another dimension to the learning process. It is well-documented by Goodlad (1979) when he describes the scheme set up at Pimlico School as part of a Community Service Volunteers project. He says in a later book that a widely-reported feature of peer tutoring is the immense personal satisfaction enjoyed by tutors and that the 'experience of being wanted can contribute to personal growth'. (Goodlad and Hirst, 1989).

Some of the reasons for introducing peer tutoring are that it is:

● a means to reinforce learning,

● a collaborative experience,

● a means of giving increased teaching.

There are other benefits. Hansen (1986) reports two studies that show that with the lessening of tension that occurs in the tutoring situation, anxiety is dispelled and the collaborative teaching produces greater 'pleasantness'. Peer pressure, too, may influence learning and the child becomes much more an active participant in his or her own progress. It has frequently been noticed by those watching children at work together that children can clarify points that the teacher has failed to get across. Increase in self-esteem and self-confidence are other advantages that observers have noticed in those doing the tutoring. It has also been of benefit in changing attitudes towards school and hence, frequently has resulted in changed behaviour.

Osguthorpe and Scruggs (1986) looked at work done on these ideas and were encouraged to set up schemes using the learning disabled, those with behaviour problems and the mentally retarded as tutors. They concluded that special education students can also function 'effectively as tutors if they are trained and supervised appropriately', and that they benefit in the ways mentioned, socially and academically, as both tutor and tutee.

Peer tutoring and literacy

A major area in which research has occurred is in the schemes set up to improve literacy skills. From the earliest accounts of tutoring, the first priority seemed to be to set up schemes for those who found reading difficult. The ability to communicate, orally and with the written word, is essential to nearly everyone and without this, children fall further and further behind. Most projects use children to teach children, as it is generally easiest to organise, especially within one school.

Many of the projects set up in America are based on extremely carefully structured programmes. The activities and the structure are prescribed, and the rewards and progress are built in. Study skills programmes, Homework Helpers programmes, Reading Workshops such as SRA and Maths worksheets are just some of the methods used. Data have indicated that the programme is a factor that contributes to the major improvements in the reading achievements of minority students. This is shown in the structured tutoring methods used in Pocoima School, California (Gartner *et al.*, 1971). Hansen (1986) showed that within the structure, there must be room for growth and change. She delivered a very structured programme for improving the vocabulary retention of seventh grade pupils working collaboratively. She admits, however, that much more than the structure was at work: the enthusiasm and challenge, and the use of oral language, must have played significant roles.

It can be seen from these few examples that there are many factors involved, some of which are difficult to evaluate. The overriding impression, however, is positive and the wealth of research finds many gains in a number of different areas. Reading, whether as the subject of a tutoring programme, or as the concern of educationalists, is always open to debate. However, most would agree with Boettcher (1978) when she said that, particularly at the secondary level, a remedial reading programme would be based on the philosophy that:

● freedom and structure are required
● involvement is essential
● success breeds success

These qualities would seem to be inbuilt in the programmes involving approaches such as paired reading (see Chapter 2) and the scheme, 'Pause, prompt and praise', both of which have been used as the basis of recent tutoring programmes.

Involvement is an essential characteristic of any learning programme. Students need to be actively involved in the learning process, as is shown by the work of Bruner, Piaget and others. Students need to be motivated, but also they need to actively engage in what they are doing: concentration is very important. To increase this, it is obvious that the more individual contact there is, the better will be the attention. Parental involvement is one way of achieving this and is very successful in many cases, but often more help needs to be given in school to improve the reading. Tutoring can provide this opportunity. Not only is there more chance for practice, but also there is active engagement between the tutor and the tutee.

Paired reading projects

In 1983 a project was set up in Kirklees, which was to help schools set up Paired Reading programmes. Of all the methods used, this one has perhaps the most positive active engagement by the two involved. Topping (1987 and 1988) describes this programme which is based on modelling, active involvement, positive reinforcement, instant feedback, selection of high interest materials and greater time involved in the act of reading. Topping (1989) reported that the best results occurred if the reading ages of the cross-age tutors were not too far apart from their tutees. Generally it was found that the tutees benefitted most, though significant improvement has been found in both tutors and tutees.

Although Sam Winter's early results (1986) showed accelerated gains in reading accuracy and comprehension in a paired reading project, he now questions (1989) whether it is the method that is instrumental in causing the gains or simply the time on-task and the organisation and training. In his review of the literature of parental involvement, and the new extensive literature on the use of peer tutoring for paired reading, he found that it was probable that the peer tutors were more effective than parents of children with reading difficulties. He said that the tutees felt more comfortable being helped by other children than by parents or teachers and that significant gains for the tutees were often matched by similar gains for the tutors.

Mary Kennedy (1989) on the other hand, in a controlled experiment using fifteen year olds tutoring eleven or twelve year olds, found a vast improvement in the reading of the tutors, and significantly less for the tutees.

Results of other methods

Earlier work, using other methods for the tutoring of reading, also shows considerable cognitive gains, not to mention the affective and behavioural effect. Graves (1977) reported a programme set up to compensate for the seriously deficient reading skills of secondary pupils. It was found that seventeen of the twenty five students tested made gains at at least twice the average rate, but the importance of the structure and organisation was emphasised. These last two points seem to be the strongest thread through all the writing on peer tutoring.

It would seem in looking at all the literature on peer tutoring that the general consensus is that it is effective. This is well-documented as I have indicated. The goals in each may be different, the purposes for the use of the method are varied, the problems to be overcome are significant, particularly in organisational terms, but most people would still agree with Thelen (1969) when he says, 'the educators, almost to a man, feel that tutoring works. I can think of no other way.'

At a recent International Conference on peer tutoring, the final plenary session stressed the importance of using 'learning by learning' to facilitate and increase the opportunities for students in a wide range of subjects to help others and thus improve themselves. The power of this experiential learning was stressed. The conference addressed the question of why the use of peer tutoring had not become more widespread and it was felt that the difficulties of organisation, the fear of change and perhaps of losing control contributed to some of the reluctance to experiment with this method in primary and secondary schools and even in colleges of higher education. Goodlad and Hirst (1989) suggest that the reluctance of professionals to believe that their work can be aided by non-professionals could be part of the problem and they conclude by saying:

> All the indications from the studies that have been made of peer tutoring in education are that the tutors will not only gain immense satisfaction from their roles, but will also learn by teaching.

There can, therefore, be no feeling that the tutors are wasting their time and it is certainly well-documented that the tutees make considerable gains.

Practical use of peer tutoring for improving children's literacy

At the beginning of this chapter I mentioned that I had been using peer tutoring in the classroom for a long time. So why, one might ask, is it necessary to do anything more than use it in this ad hoc way? The answer is perhaps evident in the brief review of the literature that I have given. To get the best results, considerable organisation is needed. For the approach to be successful the pupils need to be matched carefully; they need to be encouraged and watched as they work; time and space needs to be found for the tutoring to take place.

To illustrate a practical use of peer tutoring in school, I will describe a research project in which I was engaged. The aims were:

- to raise the reading age of those who were still struggling in the first year of their secondary school;
- to increase their confidence;
- to give senior pupils the opportunity to undertake some valuable voluntary work;
- and, incidentally, to raise the reading competence of some of the tutors.

The method to be used by the tutors for the teaching was paired reading. This method has been described in detail elsewhere in this book. It was considered the most suitable method for several reasons. It allowed freedom of choice of the reading materials: the only limitation was that the tutor should be able to read the material chosen. It encouraged a considerable amount of praise: something that most poor readers are rather short on. It was a new approach to most tutees who had been struggling with the complexities of the written word for a long time.

An appeal was made to the fourth year pupils for volunteers to work as reading tutors. Research has shown that the tutor should be about two years ahead of the tutee in reading competence so that it would be possible to choose tutors from the same academic year as the tutees.

From the enormous response, tutors were selected after they had read a detailed account of the project, attended a training session and signed an agreement. This weeded out the less serious volunteers. It is very important that there is a real commitment to the scheme by the tutor because most of those to be tutored have suffered considerable failure and are poor in organisation. They need someone who will help them in both these areas and failure to turn up to an arranged meeting will be very harmful. The tutees will often need chasing because their very failure at reading is often symptomatic of other areas of difficulty.

The goals of the scheme had to be made evident, not only to the tutors but also to the tutees. Their willingness to participate was essential to the success of the peer tutoring. If the scheme can be seen as something very important in the school, mentioned in Assembly, visited by the Head and staff from all areas of school life, it will be a great encouragement to those taking part and lead to a greater success rate.

The tutors and tutees were thus selected and matched, not quite at random. Personalities were taken into account and it proved helpful if tutors who were friends worked with tutees from the same form and thus from the same geographic situation in the school

Further training was then given to all the participants in which the following points were particularly stressed to the tutors. They were told of the necessity of:

- building confidence with a lot of praise;
- building a good relationship;
- using this opportunity for the tutee to make a fresh start with a new approach;
- discussing the text to ensure comprehension is occurring.

The pupils were shown how to use paired reading techniques and were encouraged to use this approach at least some of each session, as this technique emphasises the development of fluency and confidence. The tutors needed a lot of practice both with each other, with an experienced adult and then with their tutees. Those pupils who showed that they had developed a good relationship and had mastered the art of the paired reading were praised and left to continue. Others needed more individual tuition. The appropriate readability of the books was important in the learning stages. It proved not to be helpful if the book chosen was so easy that the tutee could read it easily, independently. Once the tutoring was established, the pairs were allowed to choose for themselves from a wide range of material, both fiction and non-fiction and, indeed, sometimes even pop magazines.

The books could be changed as often as they liked. A special box was provided in which to keep the books, suitably named and book-marked, so that it was easy to get started at the beginning of each new session. The books were meant to stay in school because they could easily be forgotten if taken home. They were frequently too difficult for independent reading and they had been specially chosen by the tutor and tutee together.

Ideally the reading should happen every day. However, this is difficult to arrange in day school, primary and secondary. It is better to be realistic and do less with success than attempt too much which may lead to failure. It is quite a commitment to tutors to give up what is essentially fifteen minutes on each occasion and my experience has shown two to three times a week to be the most that can be expected.

The tutors and tutees committed themselves initially to half a term. After this period the decision to continue was with them. It is wise not to overdo the length of any project. The effectiveness of the tutoring may decline considerably and bad habits emerge. It is more successful to have a break of some weeks before recommencing the tutoring with the same pupils. The rare pair can continue successfully indefinitely.

Careful records were kept at all stages and this evaluation of the reading that was being done encouraged good practice and ensured that difficulties were dealt with as they emerged. The kinds of problems that occurred were to do with:

- over-bossiness of a tutor,
- lack of space in the designated reading areas,
- pupils being required for practices of all kinds by other staff,
- inappropriate choice of reading matter.

However, despite these small areas of difficulty which could normally be solved, and the time required for the organisation, there is evidence to suggest that tutoring can improve reading ability; and that it can certainly increase the self-confidence of both tutors and tutees while at the same time being an enjoyable experience.

Implications for children with literacy difficulties

It could be seen by the enthusiasm engendered that it would be logical to extend this approach to other areas of difficulty such as spelling and writing. More important, it was evident that there were almost countless possibilities for using less able tutors to tutor younger pupils: thus giving the less able tutors the opportunity to improve not only their skills but also their self-confidence. Cognitive benefits for both tutor and tutee are well-documented.

Many people can cite experiences which convince then that they have benefited significantly on the occasions when they had to explain a complex subject to a friend, colleague or young person. The process of ordering ideas in order to clarify them undoubtedly results in more profound knowledge of what is being taught. This has conceptual advantages for the instructor, as well as helping the learner. It has been suggested that certain non-cognitive effects are also fairly reliably present. These have to do with responsibility, learning about learning and thus establishing an empathy with teachers, and the personal and social skills of both tutors and tutees. In terms of motivating children to take some responsibility for their learning, tutoring seems to be very successful.

The potential for tutoring would thus seem to be limitless. The strategy often adopted in sessions gives opportunities for over-learning which would be very useful in areas where the acquisition of basic skills is essential to further learning. There can be no such thing as too much learning.

As a result of co-ordinating and introducing a tutoring programme, the teacher achieves greater autonomy, and freedom from the restrictions imposed in controlling a large class. There is them time to concentrate on individuals and to concentrate on the learning process. Thus the teacher can feel that the time spent in organisation is very worthwhile.

CHAPTER 4

Aspects of Effective Classroom Management

Philip Jones

> The scene is a small open courtyard within a school building, there are paving stones, warm in the sunshine and tubs of bright flowers. On top of a low wall a child is lying, propped up on her elbows, looking at a book with intense concentration. Near her another child is carefully watering the flowers, while a third is sitting with his back against the wall and a notebook on his knees. He appears to be drawing or writing something in a book, like the first child he is lost in the task. (Donaldson, 1978)

When I first read Donaldson's description of a visit she had made to a school I was immediately attracted to the situation she had described. The implicit independence and autonomy of the children, with children surrounded by stimulating objects and children being allowed to follow their own interests, 'lost in the task', is a memorable achievement to aim for.

I aim to make my classroom interesting and stimulating for children, parents, visitors and myself. I fill the classroom with real things: skulls, clothes, machines, objects relating to themes/topics. We are surrounded by objects that provide starting points for talk, drawing, painting, writing, for exploring. The display of fish skeletons in the classroom has been used as a starting point for work in a range of curricular areas. First hand experience with these objects has provided a starting point for writing, for making books that can be used as a classroom resource. These books contain a vocabulary that is familiar and a sentence structure which the children use themselves.

This is particularly important for children with literacy problems. There is an interaction between writing and reading that is rooted in purpose and meaning.

We spend a lot of time in the classroom and we want to feel comfortable and stimulated. I want the room to be aesthetically pleasing and practical so things in the room must be well ordered. Because of practical considerations I have to control myself; I cannot go on filling our working area with artifacts as movement around the room, storage areas, and retrieval of resources must all be considered. The organisation of space and resources must promote and sustain both independence and autonomy in the children. There will be times when I need to hear children read, to work with a group, to be involved in assessment procedures and therefore uninterrupted periods will be necessary. It is important for children to realise this; it is also important for my classroom organisation to support child independence.

Curriculum organisation

I start the day with a programme of about ten activities that cover a range of curricular areas. This programme is written up on large sheets of paper on the flip chart. The activities are determined by:

- Termly and weekly planning
- Development stages of children and their individual needs
- Needs of the group
- Child initiated work
- Ongoing work.

There is also a range of activities that are available to the children (listening to tapes, language and number games etc.) I always aim to have available more activities than I really need, but this is dependent on having the available space.

Children are allocated to specific activities within the programme. I usually do this before the children come in because I need to do it properly:

(1) It is important that the children have access to a broad-based curriculum and a curriculum that meets their needs. There are also social considerations.

(2) It is important that I set myself realistic goals in terms of my interaction with the children. I may also have to integrate into my programme any child initiated themes that are introduced.

When the children come in we meet in a centrally positioned area and discuss the programme of activities that are available. Using this list of activities is useful for a variety of reasons:

- It provides a focus for the whole group.
- It provides a whole group reading activity (where I can adjust the vocabulary, the structure, to suit my audience).
- It provides real reasons for writing and reading and a context for developing a range of reading skills.

For children with specific literacy problems I can, if necessary, focus on developing:

- directionality
- word and letter boundaries
- letter recognition
- graphophonic association
- conventions such as spacing, punctuation, etc.

I can let those children who are good readers help those who do not read so well.

I also explain to the children who I will be working with, I discuss as much as possible in whole group situations so that I am left to work with a focus group or individual child.

Classroom organisation

The classroom is organised into well defined curricular areas. There are areas resourced for:

- Language work
- Mathematics
- Science (tools, bench, glues, range of materials etc.)
- Technology
- A listening area, with tapes
- A writing area (a range of tools, wordbanks, book-making materials)
- computer
- Small private book area
- An area for painting, claywork etc.
- A teaching table where I work with a focus group
- A large public area used for whole group meetings; this area is resourced with artifacts, displays related to themes and topics,

reading materials, postcards and slide collections. This area is also used for private and small group reading.

The arrangement of the furniture allows the children to work in pairs, small groups, whole group and alone. Working areas are screened off to provide privacy. (I don't want to see all the children, neither do I want all the children to see me.) The cross-curricular nature of the primary curriculum is reflected in the arrangement and use of furniture and resources.

Systems of storage and organisation of equipment are discussed and explained frequently to the children. Setting up a classroom follows distinct stages.

(1) The first stage is arranging the classroom space into curricular areas and then resourcing these areas. I give a lot of time to this first stage.
(2) The next stage is to try out the arrangements with the children and be prepared to let the classroom evolve to meet the needs of both children and teacher. I don't expect to get the arrangement right at the first attempt and the arrangement of furniture and resources may require frequent change to meet the changing needs of the children. See plan of classroom (Figure 4.1).

Expectations

I have expectations which I make clear to the children from the beginning of our period of time together. These expectations cover a range of situations and are frequently reinforced with the whole group, small groups or sometimes with individuals. I try to share and explain with the children the importance of these necessary routines. I work hard to get the children to organise materials, space and resources. I encourage the children to be independent through example and discussion; we discuss:

- Storage, maintenance of materials/resources and curricular areas in class.
- Safe and proper use of tools.
- Working in groups, working alongside other children.
- End of playtime routines; moving round the room.
- Sharing space and resources.
- Alternatives to using me as a resource.
- What to do when a piece of work is finished.

43

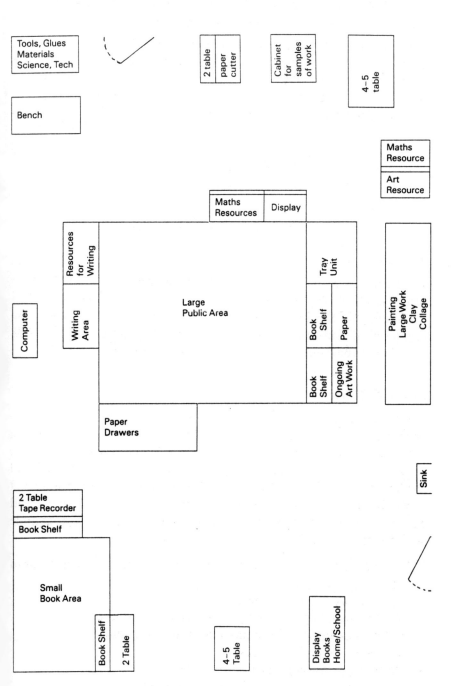

Fig. 4.1 Plan of Classroom
Approx. size $7\frac{1}{2}$ m × $7\frac{1}{2}$ m

If I am reading with a child the other children in class know I need some uninterrupted time, they know to ask help from someone else or to get a tray of books from a reading area until I am available. I am happy for the children to sit and read or talk or explore/handle the artifacts. At most times during the day children will be doing this, which serves a double purpose. I gain time to implement my plans and the children are relaxed, enjoying their environment.

There are times when I have to discuss with individual children their patterns of behaviour. When I do this I usually:

> Choose an appropriate time and place.
> Describe the behaviour specifically.
> Express my feelings about their behaviour.
> Ask for specific changes in their behaviour.

Planning

Studies of successful schools have shown the effect that good planning can have on pupil attainment.

Planning is an important characteristic of successful classroom organisation and management. The diagram (Figure 2) is a useful framework for devising termly or half termly planning.

Example of termly planning

Theme: The Clothes Show, Spring Term 1990

Priorities

- Equal Opportunities
- Multicultural aspects
- Special Educational Needs
- Green Issues/Conservation

Needs within the class:

(1) Developing/extending social skills, working alone, in small and large groups, sharing resources and space.
(2) Developing/extending literacy skills; for selected children, activities related to developing specific language skills. Reading; encourage using a range of reading strategies. Writing; developing independence.
(3) Developing/extending independence and autonomy.

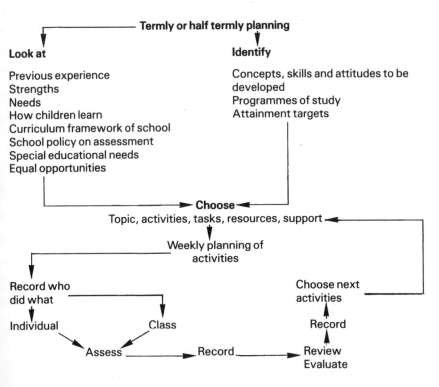

Fig. 4.2
(Adapted from ILEA Planning Document 1989)

(4) Extend keyboard/computer experience/expertise.
(5) Physical Education; develop and extend a range of skills in games, gymnastics, movement.

Starting Points:

– Collection of shoes, clothes, hats, bags, accessories . . . display.
– See below for alternative starting points.

National Curriculum Attainment Targets and Levels:

English: All attainment targets will be covered at varying levels. AT's 1, 2, 3, 4, 5.

Science:

AT1 Exploration of Science
AT6 Types and uses of materials
.1 squashed and stretched

    .2   similarities/differences
    .3   heating and cooling.

AT13   Energy
    .2   hot and cold
    .3   temperature

AT4   Genetics and evolution.
    .1   variation in human beings.
    .2   measure simple differences between each other.
    .3   life forms and extinction.

AT2   Variety of life
    .1   variety of living things.
    .2   plants and animals/sustain life.
    .3   similarities; sorting into groups, seasonal changes.

Mathematics:

AT1 + 9 Using and applying mathematics.
AT2 Understanding number and number notation.
AT3 Understand number operations.
AT4 Estimate and approximate in number.
AT8 Estimate and measure quantities.
AT10 Recognise and use properties of 2D/3D shapes.
AT12/13 Collect, record, process data, represent and interpret data.

See NC Folder for details of AT's.
AT's related to Programmes of Study.

Extension:

Favourite clothes, buying clothes, size of clothes.
Labels for clothes, washing, material content, size etc.
Colour, dyeing, printing (observational work leading to print making).
Decorations: application of colour, checks, stripes, spots, plains, patterns, etc.
Sewing, knitting, weaving.
Materials/fabrics – wools, silks, denim, etc.
Sources of raw materials.
Fur, implications.
Clothing for special occasions, sports, weddings, beaches.
Best clothes, fashion, specialist clothing, waterproofing, fireproofing, climatic variation, pyjamas, etc.
Clothes and seasons, temperature, warmth, protection.

Fastenings: buttons, toggles, zips, velcro, belts, etc.
Toys: clothes for dolls, size, scale, measures.
Accessories: shoes, trainers, gloves, hats, scarves, jewellery, spectacles, sunglasses, etc.
Function and design: taking clothes apart, nets, 2D shapes forming 3D clothes.
History: fashion, protection, survival (from what?)
Multicultural aspects; clothing, tradition, religion.
Equal opportunities: uniform.
Displays: wide range of resources available including hats, shoes, clothing and accessories.
Dressing up, fantasy, role play.
Books: The Long Blue Blazer, Jeanne Willis & Susan Varley
Beaver Books 1989
The Emperor's New Clothes, Anderson, Traditional
Mrs Mopple's Washing line, Hewitt and Bloomfield,
Puffin 1966
You'll Soon Grow Into Them Titch, Pat Hutchins,
Puffin 1983
The Little Girl and The Tiny Doll, E. Ardizonne,
Young Puffin
The Paper Bag Princess, Munsh, Hippo 1980
Mrs Lather's Laundry, Ahlberg and Amstutz,
Puffin Books/Viking 1981

Record keeping

An important part of this framework is assessment and record keeping. Assessment is a central part of my teaching. I use a range of informal and formal assessment techniques.
Assessment enables me to:

- Identify the starting points, initial levels of attainment for each pupil.
- Prepare schemes of work within the programmes of study for pupils at different levels.
- Monitor and record the AT's studied by individual children and level of attainment achieved.

Assessment should be:

- Formative to provide information that will help make decisions about how pupils' learning may be taken forward.

48

- Summative to provide a picture of overall achievement.
- Evaluative to indicate where there needs to be further effort/a change in the curriculum.
- Informative to help communication with parents.

I use a weekly record system designed in line with a set of criteria which was developed by the Working Party on Record Keeping and Assessment at my present school. This set of criteria is included below.

Planning for each week's work is closely linked with record keeping and assessment and facilitated by the use of this weekly diary, (a copy of the front page of which is included below). Further sheets are used to record the children's participation in activities, progress, development and levels of attainment within the National Curriculum. I include extracts from one child's profile from this planning/record keeping document.

Agreed criteria for weekly records

(1) A3 paper/easy to handle store, ring binder
Accessible at all times.
All childrens' names should be included.
Days of the week must be shown/dates.

(2) A breakdown of skills/activities/grouping
Space allowed for
- foundation subjects
- 3 core subjects
as well as column for permanent fixtures e.g. reading
- room for comment – individual
- room for evaluation – individual
- matching work to children/differentiation
- resources, materials needed
- AT's to be covered – progression of skills
- a colour coding to show extra curricular activities
- a weekly evaluation of self/class
- time
- an inclusion from support teacher is used.

Extracts from one Child's Education Profile: Alex

Teacher's notes for action	Teacher's observations	Parent's comments
Illustrations with label – child needs to reinforce understanding	Started washing activity with Cathy. Pre-activity questions caused problems(?) Alex not very confident leading this activity. No notes taken. Extend his social patterns in class.	Alex not choosing books by himself – relies on Mum. Unfamilar words: he often sits and waits. What cues and strategies does he use?
Checklist of clothes		
+ / − operations with numbers to 100		
65 = 6t 5 units (Needs encouragement to use apparatus)	Worked with James on Mutant Turtle Book. Brilliant illustrations. Handwriting inconsistent.	

The extracts above are taken from the weekly on-going diary.
They are a selection of the comments and observations made over a period of 3 weeks on one child as he works in a variety of curricular areas. Together these comments build up a picture of how this child is operating, what the child's needs are. They are comments that help the teacher to design a programme of activities that will meet and develop the needs of the individual child.

The weekly diary that we use is a vital tool for building up a bank of information about individual children and their starting points, initial levels of assessment. There is adequate scope for recording the National Curriculum Attainment targets studies by each pupil and when we feel an attainment target has been achieved.

Next curricular activities planned for Alex

- Activities that focus on developing a consistent handwriting style.
- Involvement in group work, working with ten rods and units, on addition and subtraction.
- Structured reading activities/informal assessment (running records/miscue analysis.) Focusing on the skills, strategies, cueing systems Alex uses.
- Greater involvement in group work to develop/extend social patterns.

The planning, preparation and delivery spiral starts again and takes learning to a new level.

EXAMPLE OF WEEKLY PLANNING

STARTING POINTS:
Fictions – *Paper Bag Princess. Mrs Lather's Laundry*
Children's clothes, sizes, labels
Fabrics, yarns, washing garments   Child initiated work

TOPIC CONTENT	CONCEPT/SKILLS	ORGANISATION
Number: Concept of Time $\frac{1}{2}$, 1, 3, 5 minutes 5, 10, 15, 20 seconds Based on *P. B. Princess* and *Mrs. Lather's Laundry* SURVEYS: What are people wearing this week? Recording data, interpreting data, PAPER BAG GARMENTS TO FIT SORTING yarns for texture: Rough/smooth, warm/cold: recording WASHING a garment: Use of detergents/various washing with warm and cold water. Instructions on labels: recording Language development. Inside and outside of garments PORTRAITS: Full scale portraits focusing on clothes. PRINTMAKING, WEAVING, KNITTING What are Polyester and Acrylic? Why are they used so much? Recording. Develop fantasy elements?	Time, time passing Days of week Telling time Co-ordination Colour/texture idea of woven fabrics, idea of rows, stitches etc.	 Children need a workable format framework/ ticksheet Small groups/ whole group for reporting back Small groups individual small groups
NON-TOPIC CONTENT		
NUMBER: Sharing/multiplication addition/subtraction. Child initiated work HANDWRITING Improving the quality of the content of books. Composition: Helping the child to say what they really mean to say. Providing real contexts for writing. PAINTING		 Organising, using dry/wet paints, choice of paper, vary brushes. Tidy up. Routines

Effective classroom management and organisation

Starting points: real things to touch, see, handle.
Space to move around without distraction.
Space to gather as a whole class.
Space for children to interact collaboratively in small groups, pairs, individually, without visual distraction.
Defined curriculum areas.
Ordered resources/attention to detail, the look of the place.
Systems, easily understood, that facilitate children's autonomy, good work habits, tidiness.
Evidence of a teacher's agenda in planning/structure/quality of intervention/expectation.
Evidence of sustained, extended, teacher interaction.

CHAPTER 5

Dyslexia – Have We Got the Teaching Right?

Jean Augur

In any class of children there will be those who:

- *positively thrive with* any teaching method;
- *adapt to and learn with* any teaching method;
- *survive in spite of* the teaching method;
- *sink or struggle because of* the teaching method.

Among the children found in the last group will be those commonly referred to as dyslexic. Such children are an enigma. While appearing to be alert and intelligent in many respects, they have extreme difficulty in acquiring literacy skills. The bewildered teacher, often anxious to help them by offering *more* of the same treatment which has already failed them, only succeeds in exacerbating the problem. Dyslexic children then begin to feel themselves failures, and what is worse, are often labelled as failures. Yet it is not the children who are failures but the teaching methods employed.

Is it possible, therefore, to change the methods of teaching and the entire environment so that those who might sink are given a chance to survive at least, and, more hopefully, to succeed?

The word dyslexia is really a misnomer. Taken literally the word translates as 'difficulty with the lexicon', which in turn has given rise to many inadequate definitions. Of these the poorest refer only to 'reading retardation', while the rather better ones refer also to spelling and occasionally to mathematics. Yet these areas comprise only a small part of the dyslexic child's profile. Equally important are his inability to label objects or people, to hear and recognise rhymes, to remember things in order, to organise himself and his work, to copy accurately, to tell the time, and to find his way from place to place. At best, the dyslexic child is seen as vague, slow, low average, a plodder who tries hard, is good with his hands but does not listen, is forgetful, and a worry. At worst, he is regarded as a slow reader, an appalling speller, thick, dumb, idle, stupid, careless, inattentive, lacking in both concentration and application, with a mother who thinks he is a genius and teacher who does not agree. The dyslexic child and his family are often under a great deal of stress.

NOTE: Throughout this chapter the male pronoun is used when referring to the dyslexic child, since four times as many boys are dyslexic as girls.

Early diagnosis

It is vitally important to identify the dyslexic child before he even enters school. This is not always easy because many of the traits or actions observed in the child's pre-school years which might, with hindsight, prove to be indicators of dyslexia, are virtually indistinguishable from those which can be seen in other children who subsequently turn out not to be dyslexic. However, it is the intensity of the trait, the clarity with which it may be observed and the length of time over which it persists, which give the vital clue to identifying the dyslexic learner.

Teachers and carers of all pre-school children should have had, in their training, input which has provided them with a good knowledge and understanding of general development. In addition, they should have been taught how to observe and record anything which may be considered unusual or enigmatic for whatever reason. This information should then be passed on to the First School on entry. Too often there is nothing in a child's school profile about his pre-school years. For many children and in particular the dyslexic child, information about his acquisition of language, ability to label, sense of rhyme and rhythm, strengths and weaknesses should all be noted, recorded and passed on when the child progresses to the next stage.

54

Two pre-school histories

(1) *Boy now aged 5 years 6 months who has been at school for 8 months:*

 - Early, clear, unhesitating speech.
 - Remembers labels i.e. names for objects and people.
 - Early ability to label all colours.
 - At three years old, he pointed to 'M' on a car number plate and said 'That's MacDonalds'. Even though the MacDonalds logo has a stylised capital 'M', he had been able to make the connection between the two shapes and the name 'MacDonalds'.
 - At four years old he stated that 'hat', 'cat' and 'fat' rhymed with each other, and that the last two letters of each word were the same. Dyslexic children of 6 years seem unable to do this.
 - At five-and-a-half he is reading from his early school readers and can spell his name and many other three-letter words by *naming* the letters.

(2) *Girl aged 3 years*:
 - Family history of dyslexia.
 - Early lisp – said 'duck*th*', 'book*th*', and 'bike*th*'.
 - Chatters incessantly but has very unclear and indistinct speech.
 - Did not crawl.
 - Appears to be a quick thinker and doer.
 - Mixes up many words and phrases in speech e.g.
     'tebby dare' for 'teddy bear';
     'Mishyhell' for 'Michelle';
     'pay the pilano' for 'play the piano';
     'cobblers club' for 'toddlers club'.
 - Great difficulty naming colours although she can point to the correct colour in response to a given label.
 - Cannot yet say any nursery rhymes.
 - Mixes up directional words, e.g. in/out, and up/down.
 - Favourite toys are – knobs, knockers, switches, plugs, the TV remote control box, the computer keyboard, and a tin of screws, nuts and bolts.
 - She trips and falls over nothing at all.

While many small children have similar profiles, experience over 30 years of observing young children has shown me that the latter is the type of child who should be observed and monitored very carefully.

suspect that when this child starts school she might be one of those who does not make the progress which her parents and teachers would expect and hope to see.

There are, of course, many well-documented reasons for children's failure to learn to read at school but the difference with the dyslexic child is that his failure is unexpected. This is a cause of great frustration to his teachers, his parents and himself.

How can the teacher help?

In view of the demands of the National Curriculum, it may be appropriate to look at the ways of helping the dyslexic child at the early stages in respect of the Attainment Targets for English – levels 1, 2 and 3. Given understanding with appropriate intervention and teaching, the majority of children including the dyslexic child will be able to take a full and active part in the new curriculum. It is the teachers' responsibility to:

13

- recognise the need
- provide appropriate intervention and teaching.

Speaking and listening

Some dyslexic children will do very well in this Attainment Target, inasmuch as they are able to enjoy stories which are read to them, and can indeed re-tell those stories accurately and with good vocabulary. Yet they may be slow to read for themselves and in that sense they will be the 'unexpected under-achievers'.

Others will find relating even a familiar story very difficult. Labelling or word-finding will be a problem. The child will need 'thinking time' to find the elusive words, and this will require patience on the part of the listener. It will be tempting for the listener to jump in and answer for him, which is very frustrating for the child. Given time, he may well find the word for himself, which will be much more satisfactory for him.

The teacher may well be aware at this time of the 'near missers'. These are children who mislabel, often choosing a word with some obvious association with the correct word e.g. 'referee' for 'umpire', 'question-mark' for 'comma'. These responses must be treated in a positive way. The child must not be told that his answer is wrong, but rather that it is a near miss and that the reasoning behind the proffered response is understood. If his responses are negatively and

56

peremptorily treated, he will soon decide to opt out of discussion for fear of rejection and ridicule.

In relating stories, such children often lose the thread of the tale. The child will ramble off in myriad directions, frequently missing the main point. Sequence and ordering of thoughts may be a problem. Such children may require visual clues. The child could follow a series of pictures set out in the sequence of the story, thereby obtaining his understanding of the order of events from those pictures.

Much work will also be needed at this stage for the child who finds the concept of rhyming difficult. Games and activities to encourage this could be devised e.g.

(1) I spy something sounding like – 'cat'.
(2) Listening for the odd one out – 'cat, 'mat', 'sack'.
(3) Listening for rhyming and non-rhyming pairs – 'cat/mat', 'cat/dog', 'log/dog'.
(4) Sorting pictures – All the pictures which rhyme with 'cat' in one box; all those which rhyme with 'pin' in another box.

The teaching and over-learning of nursery rhymes, jingles, songs, with days of the week, numbers, months, and seasons need to be consistent. Body movements should be involved as much as possible as an aid to memory.

One of the most difficult of all the speaking and listening attainments at all levels is 'responding appropriately to simple instructions given by the teacher'. This begins very early in Level 1. Dyslexic children have very poor auditory sequential memories and instructions are quickly forgotten. It will be necessary for an instruction which is given to the class as a whole to be repeated to him individually. He may have difficulty understanding the language of the instruction as well as the *message*. He should therefore be encouraged to repeat the instruction. This will serve three purposes:

(1) The teacher will know that he has heard and understood the language of the instruction.
(2) She will know that he has understood the message.
(3) The child's *own* voice is his best mnemonic and will aid his recall mechanism.

N.B. The instruction 'Tell me your address' does *not* mean 'Say, "I am a dress" ', as the dyslexic child might suppose!

Level 3 demands the retelling of a story in sequential order with a beginning, a middle and an end. It will be necessary to check whether the child with directional difficulties understands the labels 'beginning', 'middle' and 'end'. Again, the picture sequences may be necessary with the following questions being posed:

- Where does the story start?
- What happens first?
- What happens next?
- What is the most exciting part?
- How did it end?

Reading

Since the 1950's, the methods generally used for the teaching of reading have been and still are those based on a visual approach. Originally, the most common terms employed were 'whole-word', 'look-and-say' or 'the sentence method'. More recently, expressions such as 'reading for meaning', 'emergent reading' and 'real books' have come into common use. Although based on the work of the psycholinguistic theorists, these are all nevertheless, variations of the visual approach, with a common underlying assumption that children learn to read from reading. Surprisingly perhaps, since there seems to be no a priori reason why this should be so, many children do in fact learn to read in this way, and it is odds-on that indeed this is the way in which the theorists themselves learned to read.

Unfortunately, a substantial number of children do *not* respond to such methods, while the dyslexic child, in particular, is totally bewildered by them. He appears to have a very small memory bank for whole words which he quickly forgets. New words are not stored in the memory very easily or for very long, and even words once retained, drop out of memory very soon if that retention is not reinforced by frequent recall and use. Such children are known as 'quick-forgetters'. Children's comments when confronted by a page of text are: 'I wish the words would stay in my head' or 'The word's in my head but I can't get it out'. These are very common remarks.

It is obvious too that similar looking or similar sounding words are a source of confusion e.g.

Brown/down; glen/clan; looks/books; one/once.

No one would deny that it benefits all children to have a background of the written word. It is well documented that, in general, where children have been regularly read to pre-school, and where children and parents read together, the results are found to be beneficial.

Unhappily for the dyslexic child, in spite of such a background, he still has very little 'book knowledge'. It is not automatic for him to know where the book starts or to scan from left to right, or to know what is meant by the terms 'word', 'sentence', 'capital letter'. He must be taught all of these things. The work of Marie Clay (1985) emphasises the importance of not making the assumption that the child has accumulated such knowledge automatically.

The child who is having difficulties will need to be read to for much longer than other children of the same age and ability. Children's literature has never been as good as it is at present, and in order to keep the dyslexic child's joy in books, it is necessary to read to him until such time as he can read for himself efficiently. Until that time comes however, there is little merit in making him struggle to read every word for himself, which will afford him little pleasure and may indeed 'turn him off' books altogether.

In the classroom, the child who is not succeeding on the method of teaching reading which is standard to that particular school, is likely to be offered help. That help is usually in the first instance 'more of the same' i.e. additional helpings or an intensification of the very approach which has already proved non-effective. When this is found still to be unsuccessful, a phonics approach may be tried. Providing that the sounds are well taught, this alternative strategy for tackling unknown words will undoubtedly help him to cope with 'regular' words, i.e. those which conform to a regular pattern of sound/letter relationships e.g.

/m/a/n e/n/d t/i/n

However, there are two main problems with a simple phonics approach. The first is that many words cannot be deciphered in this way e.g. 'said', 'bought'. The second is that the importance of the order in which the letters are introduced to the child is usually ignored. The principal reason for introducing 'sounds' is so that the child can use them as quickly as possible in meaningful words, preferably for both reading and writing.

The sounds can be introduced in one of three ways:

Firstly: alphabetical order. Unfortunately, the first five letters of the alphabet present considerable difficulties, namely;

- Two similarly sounding vowels are presented closely following one another i.e. (ă) as in 'apple', and (ĕ) as in 'egg'. This is very confusing for some children particularly those who have had early ear problems.

- There are two 'ball-and-stick' letters, 'b' and 'd', which not only look alike to many children, but also sound alike to them.
- The letter 'c' presents difficulties of its own. When placed before the letter 'a' it sounds k as in 'cat', but when put before the letter e it will sound as in 'cent'.
- The number of words which can be made out of this combination of letters is very limited, and moreover, many of these words both sound and look alike e.g. 'dad', 'add', 'bad' and 'bed'.

Secondly: Some advocate an order of introduction which groups together similarly shaped letters e.g. c, a, d, g, q. It is immediately clear however, that although this group does contain a vowel, the number of words which can be made from these letters is even more limited than with the alphabetical order.

Thirdly: Experience has shown me that a letter order which enables the maximum number of words to be built up from it as rapidly as possible, without presenting at the same time opportunities for confusion, is much to be preferred to either of the above. Such an order is that proposed by the late Kathleen Hickey (1977) for dyslexic learners, namely:

Letter	Sound
i	|ĭ| as in 'indian, 'igloo', 'ink'
t	|t| as in 'table, 'tent', 'top'
p	|p| as in 'pig', 'penny', 'pot
n	|n| as in 'not', 'nose', nut'
s	|s| as in 'sun', 'sock', 'sit'

Children learn the relationship between the sound of the letter, the letter-name, and its hand-written shape. The hand-written shape is always learned superimposed on the printed form of the letter (Fig. 5.1). Hence the child does not become confused between the letter he sees in his reading book, and form he will write in his writing book. He associates the one with the other.

Fig. 5.1

A joined style of writing, not print, is an intrinsic part of the programme.

Some of the words which can be made out of this initial combination of letters are:

Words for reading and spelling:

it	in	pips	tits
tit	tin	tips	spits
pit	pin	snips	sits
nit	spin		
spit			

Two-syllables: insist

Contraction: it's

Already a pattern begins to emerge: groups of letters which in this case both look alike and sound alike. These are regular, recurring patterns which provide early opportunity for rhyming words.

In addition, as indicated above, words with initial and final blends can be introduced, as can plurals and the use of third-person singular verbs. Contractions and two-syllable words can be made.

It will be seen therefore, that this is a very efficient group of letters with which to start. Children taught the fundamental concepts of sound, letter, written-shape relationship with these very carefully selected letters will have a much firmer foundation on which to build. Additional letters can be added as fast as possible, but as slowly as may be necessary. New words are added to the child's reading and spelling vocabulary with every new letter taught. Sight words, e.g. 'said', which is taught immediately after the introduction of the letter d, are taught by the Simultaneous Oral Spelling method first proposed by Orton in the 1920's and revised by Bradley in 1985. Whereas, with the majority of learners, reading skills are readily transferred to spelling, it appears that the dyslexic child learns more efficiently the opposite way. For him, writing and spelling skills are transferred to reading. This reflects the Montessori philosophy that we should teach children to write and read, *in that order*.

In the light of the above, I doubt if the dyslexic child will fare well with the National Curriculum Attainment Targets for reading, for the Curriculum is firmly based on the 'real books' philosophy of reading previously described. It takes little account of the children who do not learn in this way. It assumes, for example, that all children will be *reading* the word 'scissors' if they know that the scissors are in the drawer labelled 'scissors'. Yet, seeing the word 'scissors' anywhere else would probably mean nothing to the dyslexic child. If the word 'cupboard' is on the cupboard, a dyslexic child may well say 'cupboard', but if the same word appears in a book it will seem that he has never seen it before. There is no transfer of learning because he has not retained the word.

Level 2 demands knowledge of the alphabet. How does the child with poor sequencing ability remember 26 letters in order? In any case, many young children who are not dyslexic can indeed recite the alphabet by rote, but that does not mean that they understand its uses.

It is necessary to teach dyslexics very carefully the order of alphabet letters, and much over-learning will be required. Dictionary skills, too, must be taught systematically, including dictionary division and a knowledge of where the quartiles come i.e. words beginning with the letters A, B, C, D, are found in the first quarter of the dictionary, those beginning E, F, G, H, I, J, K, L, M, in the second quarter, those beginning N, O, P, Q, R, in the third, and finally those beginning S, T, U, V, W, X, Y, Z, in the last quarter.

Teachers must remember that dictionaries are meant for the meanings and pronunciation of words, *not* to find an unknown spelling. It is necessary to know accurately the first three letters of a word before a child has any chance of finding it in a dictionary. Moreover, unless the word is spelled as it sounds he may still not find it. Also, teachers should check that the word being sought is in fact in the dictionary in the first place. This may seem an obvious precaution, but all too often I have witnessed instances of children struggling to find a word that was not listed in the particular dictionary in use.

By the end of Level 2 children will be expected to 'read a range of material with some independency, fluency, accuracy, and understanding'. For the dyslexic child this is unlikely to happen. Although 'phonic cues' are mentioned there are no guidelines or helpful suggestions on the specific teaching of these cues. This is a missed opportunity, one which is going to severely hinder the dyslexic and many other children. It is well known that even though many dyslexic children remain unidentified until the ages of 8, 9 or 10, when they are given the appropriate structured language teaching, that is, improving their reading through writing and spelling, they begin to make substantial progress. If such methods were generally employed in mainstream classrooms from the very beginning, the child who is at risk from the methods presently in use would have a better chance of success, without the natural learners referred to early in this chapter being disadvantaged.

Writing

Attainment targets 3 and 5:

I have bracketed these Targets together because I believe they are properly associated, albeit that Target 3 talks of 'writing' while Target 5 speaks of 'handwriting'. The one is usually an intrinsic part of the other. If it is true that children need a reasonably flowing hand and a reasonable facility with spelling before they enjoy writing stories, why do we expect children to do so much 'creative' writing before they have acquired the necessary skills? Creativity comes from within and many dyslexic children are very creative. Unfortunately the creativity is killed stone-dead when it has to be produced in handwritten form. There is no creativity or fluency of thought if the child is required to ask for the spelling of every other word he needs.

Neither is it rewarding for the child to pour out his creative thoughts on to paper, only to find that no one can decipher his efforts. If such a child is asked to read back his work immediately, he may be able to remember what he has attempted to write, but by the next day it is doubtful whether even he would be able to decipher the piece. Other ways must be devised for him, such as providing him with a scribe.

He will need a scribe for his stories for much longer than other children of the same age and ability. Moreover, he should not then be expected to copy the story from the scribe's model. Copying is a very difficult task for dyslexics, and unless he has excellent letter formation, which is most unlikely, he will be reinforcing poor letter shapes. Indeed, some of these shapes may be so malformed that they are actually incorrect shapes, which will need to be re-taught correctly at a later date if the child is to learn an efficient joined handwriting style.

It is a great pity that print-script was ever introduced into schools. There is no evidence to support its use. According to an excellent article in the *Times Educational Supplement* in 1981 by Christopher Jarman, print-script was so designed in 1913 by the L.C.C. as an alternative to the difficult, looped, civil-service cursive style taught at that time to all children in big classes. Unhappily, its introduction did a great disservice, not only to dyslexic children, but to the nation generally. Even though children were not actually taught incorrect writing movements, they have clearly been allowed to develop such movements to the point where they become habitual, and this at the crucial learning period between 5 and 7 years. Figure 5.2 shows a good example of this.

Fig. 5.2

These movements must be 'unlearned' before the proper movements can be accurately taught. This is a total waste of time. Flowing writing follows naturally on from scribbling movements, a fact which can be harnessed to beneficial effect immediately the child enters school. Teachers are often reluctant to teach a joined style of writing on the mistaken assumption that the child will be confused between the style of letters he sees in his reading books, and the style of writing he will be doing in his writing book. This confusion simply does not arise if the child is taught in the manner suggested earlier in this chapter, i.e. by linking the sound to the letter-name and its written shape.

The simplest form of the letters is taught with linking strokes for joining strings of letters together. As soon as two letters are taught they are linked in a word. A joined style of writing not only improves speed and presentation of writing but is also an aid to spelling. Regular flowing letter-strings taught for writing and spelling then transfer to recognition for reading. The ability of children to join letters should not be underestimated. There is no need to wait until a child is 7 or 8 years old. He can start this at 5 with very beneficial results.

Spelling

Although the National Curriculum is better as regards spelling than on reading or writing, it still assumes too much. Level 1 demands that children should be able to write some letter-shapes in response to speech sounds and letter names. The teacher will therefore need to teach this relationship, and in order to do so, she must be clear in her own mind. Sounds are an aid to reading. Letter-names are necessary for spelling. Children must be taught how to spell the following:

(1) Single sounds e.g. |ĭ| – i
|t| – t
|p| – p
|n| – n
|s| – S

(2) Blends |sp| – sp
|st| – st

(3) Syllables |ĭp| – ip

(4) Small words |ĭt| – it
|ĭn| – in

Irregular words which do not spell as they sound must be taught using the Simultaneous Oral Spelling method. This is a multi-sensory method using sight, sound, voice and hand. It proceeds thus:

(1) Present the word clearly printed.
(2) Read the word to the child.
(3) Child repeats word.
(4) Child writes over the word *naming* the letters and joining the writing. This is repeated as many times as necessary.
(5) Child covers the word and writes from memory *naming* the letters as he does so.
(6) Child checks word with original.

The pat phrase 'Look-Cover-Write-Check' has not served the dyslexic child well. Cripps (1987) himself questions the terminology, suggesting that if children are simply looking at the word, they are probably reading it and not studying it for spelling. This is exactly what dyslexic children have done over the years. Hence, the methods employed by teachers to help them have in fact failed them.

It is imperative that all teachers have a good knowledge of the structure of English spelling and of the guidelines, strategies and spelling choices necessary to help the children in their classes. So often teachers have only a limited knowledge of these guidelines etc. of which the following are those most commonly taught:

(1) The magic 'e'.
(2) 'i' before 'e', except after 'c'.
(3) Change 'y' to 'i' before adding 'es'.

I suspect that these three dicta were the only ones taught to the teacher themselves when they were at school. The dyslexic child is going to need much more than these.

Teachers also need to be aware of which spelling attempts are acceptable at any given age. Children of 5 or 6 writing 'sed' for 'said', 'wnt' for 'went', 'woz' for 'was', are making appropriate attempts. They are, as Frith says, 'Reading by eye and spelling by ear'. However, similar attempts made by a bright 8-year-old are a cause for concern.

It is probably a truism that the degree of success which any child achieves with the National Curriculum will depend largely on the skill of his or her teacher. For the dyslexic child, however, this is unquestionably so. The greater the teacher's understanding of such a child's learning style, the greater will be her ability to help him. She should be able to build up a profile of the child, concentrating on his strengths as much as on his weaknesses, so that a clear picture will emerge. From this, the teacher's observations should lead naturally to appropriate intervention at the vital time.

Methods used successfully with dyslexic learners are also appropriate for many other young learners. If these methods were applied more generally in primary classrooms, there would be fewer under-achieving children subsequently requiring additional support. As for the dyslexic child in particular, there is nothing *wrong* with him. It is not the case that he has some peculiar quirk we have to straighten out. Rather, he has a different perception of things, which we must channel into. Too often, it is the teaching methods used which do not suit the dyslexic child. We must be clever enough to adapt our teaching so that he will understand and learn, for he is longing to learn and has much to offer. We can learn a great deal from him, and in so doing, we shall become much better teachers of all children.

CHAPTER 6

Helping Children
who find Writing Difficult

Helen Keene

Writing is always a complex activity needing a smooth synthesis o
many skills in order to convey the writer's meaning to another person
I did not realize just how much was involved until I had persona
experience with my own daughter. I had to help her with every aspect
including letter formation, punctuation, spelling and how to construc
a sentence. Nothing was easy for her (or for me either!) and everythin
needed constant practice and revision. This was in spite of her verba
language skills being well above average.

I have found that the ideas I used with my daughter have beer
helpful to me in the classroom. Work on handwriting and spelling
helps those who have ideas and plenty to say but cannot translate thei
creativeness into a written form that is easy for anyone else to
understand. In addition, there may be other children in the class who
appear to have little enthusiasm for anything, let alone writing. Fo
these children, in particular, it is necessary to provide a stimulating
and interesting environment in which occasions for writing will occu
naturally.

In teaching the mechanics of writing, the two aspects of spelling anc
handwriting need to be considered. Handwriting is extremely
important because the reader should not be distracted by difficulties ir
deciphering words but should be able to concentrate on the message
Children should be taught from the beginning to form letters in the
most economical and logical way in order to progress easily to a joinec

script. Many schools are now adopting a handwriting scheme for the whole school and it may be necessary for some teachers to reform their own handwriting first. With practice, it is possible for an adult to write in several different styles according to the purpose of the exercise. In trying to change their own writing style, teachers can gain a small insight into the difficulties children have when trying to re-learn a kinaesthetic skill. Just as you never forget how to ride a bicycle or even swim, old habits are very difficult to change, particularly without self-motivation. Therefore it is very important for children to learn from the beginning the conventional ways of forming and joining letters.

In addition it has been my experience that helping children to improve their writing and spelling skills also serves to encourage them to be more confident in their approach to writing. So it is worth spending time and taking the trouble to improve both the spelling and handwriting of pupils. This may mean that teachers need to make their own knowledge and understanding explicit rather than implicit so that they can explain and teach both spelling and handwriting. I have also found it helpful to make clear the purpose of these activities – 'We need to write clearly so that other people can read what we have written'. These lessons should, however, be separate and distinct from the occasions where we encourage children's own writing and the content obviously depends on the age of the children. However I do feel it is important to correct the spelling of the common words as soon as possible.

The desire to write will arise when a person sees a need to communicate through writing. Teachers need to provide opportunities and an environment where these occasions arise naturally. It encourages the children to see themselves as writers if they have access to a well laid out writing corner where pens, paper and little books are readily available. Every opportunity should be used for encouraging writing, from making birthday and 'get well' cards to notes for other people at school and home.

The kind of writing will vary according to its purpose and according to the person to whom it is addressed. If someone writes a few notes as a personal reminder, a fair copy is not necessary but once something is written for other people to read there is a need for a corrected version and children can understand this necessity. The children should be given the opportunity to discuss, revise, and redraft their work. They should be encouraged to do this with each other, as well as with the teacher. It is very important to try to make time to talk to the children about what they have written, helping them to make small steps

forward by talking about what they have written and how to bring
their version closer to a conventional version.

It is often helpful to give the opening phrase or sentence when
discussing a piece of writing. It is also important to encourage the
children to have an introduction, some development or happening and
then a conclusion. It makes later work much easier for children if they
are used to following this pattern. It needs a lot of practice to be able to
round off a piece of writing with a conclusion but I do not mean
anything elaborate by this. Often all it needs is a sentence to sum the
story up.

I find it useful to encourage personal creative writing through the
use of a combination of the children's senses. Usually a session will
begin with a verbal discussion in which the flow of ideas is stimulated
by interaction with other people. As with any group, there will always
be some who are more dominant than others. One way of neutralising
their effect may be to split the class into groups, making each of these
children responsible for a group. Ask them to take notes and give them
the responsibility for recording a contribution from each member.
These sessions are often very noisy because lots of people are trying to
talk at the same time. I usually try to calm the most excitable ones by
joining their discussion first. By the time I have visited each group it is
usually appropriate for everyone to join back together so that the
whole class can share their conclusions, using the leader a
spokesperson. Then the children can usually see the necessity for the
notes they have kept.

Sometimes it is appropriate to begin the discussions through the use
of a picture or an object. The teacher can provide these but I have
found that the children are more interested if you make a suggestion
and ask them to bring something they think is relevant. In this way the
children are involved more closely and the topic can develop in
surprising ways. It is important not to reject the children's ideas but if
you feel something is totally inappropriate, ask them to justify their
choice.

Most teachers have a very strong visual sense but for a significant
proportion of children one of the other senses dominates and for these
children it is very valuable to use these other senses.

Aural stimulation through the use of commercial or specially
prepared tapes is very easy. You can use music which suggests images
or which evokes moods to stimulate different kinds of writing, ranging
from stories to free verse. This can also be done in conjunction with
the use of pictures or objects.

To touch, as in handling an object, can also be a powerful stimulus to the imagination. I have also found that children who experience particular difficulty with reading and writing respond very well to the use of the kinaesthetic sense, which is involved in feeling and touching, so that they can base their writing on something they can handle or that they have made.

Children often find it easier to write if boundaries are set. The sense of being an observer of a restricted world can be used by making a variation on the theme of looking through an aperture. It is effective to cut a keyhole shape out of black paper and mount it on pale paper. The scene through the peephole can be shown in different ways – drawing, painting, collage, etc. It can show the inside of a room or be the view looking out. Variations on this idea can be made by using a flap as a door with a handle to open it or for an outdoor scene, a window frame with pleated tissue curtains. The theme can be based on a favourite class story or linked in to the class topic. An interesting way of bringing the writing to the whole class is to create the scene inside the aperture on tissue paper. Then if the classroom is blacked out, the scene can be illuminated by a torch while the teacher reads the story. I find it better to read the story myself in this sort of situation since it is difficult for children to read out loud to the whole group. I find it captures the interest of the listeners better when reading out loud, to use a wide variation of voice and tempo, with dramatic pauses.

Another method is to create a model that is partially two- and partially three-dimensional. A piece of card can be used as the lid of a pirate's treasure chest. By cutting round three sides and folding the fourth you can make a hinged lid which can be opened by using a piece of string attached to the front and pulled through at the back. Movement always makes things more attractive and interesting. When the lid is slowly raised, inside can be seen a priceless treasure! This can be as elaborate or as simple as you wish and again can incorporate collage as well as drawing and painting. Perhaps it is because I enjoy making collages myself that I find this way of representing objects and scenes to be the most effective with children. However, I have found that you do not need to be able to do these things very well yourself. If you provide the materials and opportunity most children will do the rest. If they work in groups they will help and encourage each other. This idea can be adapted to spaceship controls or a wizard's case. This kind of activity can be used as the starting point for different kinds of writing.

Instead of the more usual 'story' you can encourage factual writing in the form of a set of instructions. These may be linked to the discovery of the 'treasure' and can include cross-curricular links with geography (map-drawing) and mathematics (co-ordinates). For the other ideas suggested, the writing could be a logical series of instructions for using the equipment. The writers will need to put themselves in the position of someone trying to use an unfamiliar piece of equipment; a well-known source of difficulty. If the children read out the instructions to each other it will help them to see where points need to be clarified. The children can work in pairs to see if they are able to understand the instructions with the author reading out the instructions first to see if they can be followed. Again it is helpful to precede the writing by a discussion of the points that need to be taken into consideration, for example, that every detail must be mentioned.

Another activity that older children like is making shoe box theatres. Up to half the lid is cut away and the opening covered with strong coloured tissue paper. A small hole is cut in the small side of the box at the dark end and this is used to look through at the scene created inside. The possibilities with this are endless: underwater or jungle (green tissue), space (blue tissue), haunted houses (grey tissue). Moving figures can be pushed in through slits in the side and objects raised by cotton pulled through the top. Two or possibly three children can work together to produce a script to read to the viewers or which they can read for themselves. If the script is to be read by other people the children will be able to see the necessity for a fair copy with conventional spelling. Children usually enjoy producing this on the word processor. A further development would be to produce a handbook containing the story with instructions for moving the characters. Since children often find difficulty with this concept of looking at something from another person's point of view, any natural opportunity for writing in this way is very valuable.

Some children have difficulty with sequencing events when telling stories and for them the story needs to be broken down into separate and distinct stages. A visual representation of the sequence helps to reinforce the concept of the logical development necessary in a story. Most children enjoy making story boards for a class 'television' story and this is a valuable exercise for children wih sequencing problems. The story is drawn in frames like a cartoon strip and unrolled across the front of a square box. It needs to unroll from right to left so that the pictures can be drawn in natural order from left to right. It is possible for a group to produce the story, each child drawing one or two frames. The teacher needs to discuss the story line with the children and make sure all the elements are covered. I always find we have difficulty in manipulating the rollers smoothly but this doesn't seem to bother the children.

Shadow puppets are fun to make and can range from the simple to the very sophisticated. Characters are drawn on white card and coloured with felt tip pens. To make them transparent you need to rub them with a pad of cotton wool soaked in vegetable oil and after this you attach them to a rigid stick. An Anglepoise lamp is the most effective way of lighting the screen, which need be nothing more elaborate than an old sheet, although it needs to be tightly stretched. The main difficulty is usually in finding somewhere dark enough for the shadows to be easily visible. Generally the children will choose to act out a story with the puppets and they will each need a script.

The children can be encouraged to see the need for a format that everyone can easily read and the word processor is ideal for providing as many copies as necessary. Arrangements can be made to show the play to other classes thus bringing the work to a wider audience. Usually the work is shown to younger children but I have found that groups of older children can be most appreciative and very encouraging with their comments. Of course, you will lose no opportunity for writing and so a written invitation is sent, necessitating a written reply and then, of course, a 'thank-you' letter. Other members of staff are usually very amenable to setting up this sort of exercise, especially if plenty of notice is given.

All these ideas are obviously easier to incorporate into the class activities if the teacher is imaginative but I have found that the children will always expand the original idea if they are given the scope to do so. The main idea needs to be well thought out beforehand and it pays to construct a shoe-box theatre or shadow puppet at home in order to be sure that you know it will work. My instructions are not very detailed but it is easy to find craft books with similar ideas if you feel you want more information. The important aspect is to find activities from which writing will either arise naturally or can easily be encouraged.

Before you begin the activity make yourself a list – and encourage children to do the same – and have everything ready. Bring spares because children can be forgetful. If you want things brought from home, allow plenty of time. A little note (another opportunity!) written by the children may stop them announcing, 'I have got to take . . . '. Organising these kinds of projects can be difficult with a whole class in the room. It is often easier to try to start off with fewer children when there is a primary helper or parent available. Naturally

it is better to begin with the most co-operative children and usuall;
once the project starts to take shape everyone wants to join in.

Helping children to see themselves as writers can be the mos
difficult but eventually the most rewarding task for teachers. We nee

to provide an environment where the children feel happy t
experiment and where their efforts are rewarded with constructiv
criticism. It is important to respond initially to the content of th
writing. The format needs to be corrected only if it is intended fo
wider circulation. The children learn more through languag
experiences and discussion than through instruction and correction
important though these are. We need to provide a range o
opportunities for writing including those initiated by the childre
themselves. We need to help the children to have a purpose in writing
Above all, we need to understand the way in which writing skills ar
built up and be ready to help the children forward by building on wha
they already know. We must show that we value their efforts and s
help them to become more proficient in conveying their ideas throug
writing.

CHAPTER 7

Children with Spelling Problems

Nata Goulandris

There can be little doubt that poor spellers are severely handicapped. The embarrassment they suffer when the teacher, other children or they themselves are unable to read their work is negligible compared to the low self-esteem many develop as a result of their inability to participate fully in normal classroom activities. Children who cannot spell are unable to write stories, record personal news, send letters to family or friends, write shopping lists. In short, their ability to function adequately in everyday life is severely curtailed.

To enable all children to attain spelling competence, spelling instruction should be part of the curriculum throughout schooling, particularly during the early years. Teachers need to function as facilitators, evaluating a child's current need, encouraging and introducing constructive strategies and enabling the baffled child to surmount current difficulties and misunderstandings.

The ultimate aim of successful spelling instruction is 'automatic spelling' (Schonell, 1942) when a writer is able to spell words spontaneously with only occasional deliberations. Once a writer has acquired fluent spelling, it becomes possible to concentrate almost exclusively on the content and structure of expressive writing.

The traditional view of spelling considered that spelling acquisition was simply a matter of rote-learning. Hence spelling instruction consisted of learning long lists of unrelated words – a system which is still considered appropriate in some schools. More recent views of spelling regard the acquisition of spelling as complex linguistic processing during which children not only learn the spelling of individual words but simultaneously acquire generalizations about the manner in which English orthography, our spelling system, functions.

Researchers are just beginning to unravel some of the component cognitive abilities which are necessary for the smooth acquisition of correct spellings. Indeed, I believe that failure to acquire initial spelling competence will eventually be regarded as the critical diagnostic sign in the assessment of specific learning difficulties because poor spelling frequently signals existing cognitive impairments which may not be apparent if a child's reading seems to be progressing adequately.

Phoneme awareness and segmentation

Speech is composed of a series of continuous speech sounds, often referred to as 'the speech stream'. The separate speech sounds, or phonemes, are difficult to isolate in words because in running speech the phonemes overlap. Phonemic awareness, the ability to recognize phonemes and phonemic segmentation, dividing spoken words into phonemes (e.g. /c/ /a/ /t/) are, in fact, critical abilities which are necessary for the successful acquisition of reading and spelling. (Liberman *et al.*, 1977; Bradley and Bryant, 1983).

Children who have not yet acquired phonemic awareness may fail to recognize that words such as 'mother', 'man', 'monkey', 'mint' all begin with the same sound, and may be unable to identify or produce rhymes. They will be unable to segment phonemes, i.e. to isolate the individual phonemes in words. In turn, they will fail to understand the alphabetic principle which underlies the English language. This inability to discern the vital link between the speech sounds of words and the letters which represent those speech sounds will prevent a child from developing efficient word recognition and competent decoding skills. Thus, the child with faulty or impoverished phonological processing is often an inaccurate reader, is unable to decode unfamiliar words (Snowling, 1980) and fails to learn more than elementary spelling skills because he has no tools for constructing unfamiliar spellings (Frith, 1985).

Development of spelling skills

Every child who is learning to spell has at least two types of spelling knowledge (Ehri, 1985):

(1)   Word specific information held in a word store or 'lexicon'.
(2)   Orthographic knowledge, stored information and working hypotheses about how the spelling system functions.

Word specific knowledge refers to the words a child already knows how to spell. There are very few children who do not know how to spell a few words when they begin school. Children can usually write their own first name, 'Mum', 'Dad', and sometimes the names of siblings or friends.

Word specific information is thought to be held in a word store of learned spellings or 'mental lexicon' (Ellis, 1984). When a word's spelling is learned, its 'orthographic representation' that is, the letters contained in its spelling, are added to the information held in the lexicon. Once a spelling has been memorized and stored, it is normally readily obtained when required.

Orthographic knowledge is the child's current level of understanding about how the writing system functions. Children make generalizations about orthography (the spelling system) using their limited experience of written language as the data base.

As individuals accumulate more experience of written language, generalizations are likely to become more accurate. Some children, however, will fail to make valid generalizations regardless of how much exposure they have had to the printed word. These children will need comprehensive, explicit instruction in the correct patterns of English spelling.

Fortunately children's current understanding of their language's spelling system can be evaluated through their invented spellings – the spellings which they produce when they are trying to spell an unfamiliar word (Mann, Tobin and Wilson, 1987). Teachers who realize the diagnostic potential of invented spellings are more likely to notice which children are failing to acquire basic skills.

How do children acquire orthographic knowledge?

When learning to spell children make hypotheses about the way that written language works in exactly the same way as they previously made hypotheses about the rules of oral language when they were learning to speak. They revise their theories if new information indicates that their prediction was incorrect (Henderson, 1980). Many spellers initially assume that spellings are virtually transcriptions of the speech sounds in the word. Hence early spelling often relies almost exclusively on representing the sound of words, disregarding other aspects of correct spelling. Learning how letters or letter strings represent the speech sounds in words appears to be a prerequisite of spelling competence (Frith, 1985; Ehri, 1985). Children who fail to understand the fundamental relationship between letters and phonemes (speech sounds), invariably have trouble acquiring spelling skills (Snowling, 1985).

More experienced spellers eventually realize that spelling by sound is unreliable because speech sounds can be represented by alternative spelling patterns but only one spelling pattern will be correct. The short /e/ sound on the word 'bed', for example, can be spelled as 'e' or as 'ea' as in the word 'head'. In addition, many words have exceptional spellings which can never be correctly worked out when spelling by sound as, for example, in the word 'yacht'.

Proficient orthographic knowledge will eventually also incorporate:

- Knowledge about *morphemes* (the meaningful units in language such as 'mis', 'un', 'pro').
- *Lexical families*: Words which have the same meaning are spelled in the same way. The silent 'g' in sign is maintained in the words 'sign' and 'signal', while 'autumn' and 'autumnal' share the letter 'n' although it remains silent in the word 'autumn' (Stubbs, 1980)
- *Transitional Probability*: Competent spellers gradually learn to evaluate the probability of certain letters or letter strings occurring more frequently than others. For example, 'f' occurs more frequently than 'ph'; the sound of long 'a' is more frequently represented by 'ay' than by 'ey'). This type of knowledge permits us to predict unfamiliar spellings far more accurately than if we used letter sound-correspondences alone.

Young children tend to use sound-letter correspondence rules to sound out a word they do not know how to spell. Indeed many pre-school children rely on their understanding of the speech sounds in words when trying to spell, producing unconventional spellings which retain the sounds of the words remarkably well. (Chomsky, 1970; Read, 1986).

Children's initial attempts to work out new words using sound-letter rules are, however, only partially successful. Initially many children omit the vowels, representing only the consonants because consonants are easier to recognize and identify than the vowels. For example, they may spell 'close' as *clz*; 'dog' as *dg*; 'elevator' as *lvtr*; 'kangaroo' as *kngr*. The representation of vowels is gradually incorporated, but the correct spelling of both short and long vowels takes a long time to master. The short vowels, as for example the /a/ sound in 'cat', the /e/ sound in 'pet', the /i/ in 'pin', /o/ in 'pot' and the /u/ in 'fun' are confusing for inexperienced spellers and most poor spellers. Many children find it exceedingly difficult to distinguish between them unless they are given protracted training.

Another notable obstacle beginners face when spelling new words is learning how to represent long vowels, the sounds represented by the letter names, namely 'a', 'e', 'i', 'o', 'u'. At first, beginner spellers represent long vowels using the respective letter names. Accordingly, they may spell 'soap' as *sop*; 'mane' as *man* and 'sleep' as *slep*. Later they incorporate markers (additional letters which change the length of the vowel) but it frequently takes a long time before the principle of final 'e' and the use of vowel digraphs such as 'oa' and 'ew' becomes properly understood. Many teachers have rued the day they introduced the notion of the 'magic' 'e' or the 'silent' 'e' only to find that an 'e' has been added indiscriminately to any spelling of which the child is remotely unsure. Nevertheless, a child cannot learn to spell accurately without understanding implicitly or, if necessary, explicitly that long vowels require markers.

It is also possible to generate a spelling for an unfamiliar word by spelling it like a word one already knows how to spell, as for example, 'spelling 'frog' like 'dog', or 'rice' like 'mice' (Goswami, 1988). Some young children use this strategy spontaneously, finding it easier than sounding out a word sound-by-sound. The main advantage to the use of analogy when spelling is that a child is more likely to produce a spelling which conforms to English structure even if the precise spelling pattern adopted may be incorrect – e.g. 'three' spelled as 'threa' by analogy to 'tea'.

Ultimately all children must learn to spell words using conventional spellings. Consequently, children must be encouraged to learn correct spellings and should be dissuaded from relying too much on sound strategies. On the other hand, there is convincing evidence that the ability to learn spelling effectively is dependent on the establishment of competent alphabetic skills (Frith, 1985). Hence, it is wise to encourage sound strategies during the early stages of spelling acquisition if children do not yet know how to spell a word. The more complex levels of orthography and the need for accurate coding and recall of orthographic information should be stressed once children have acquired basic alphabetic skills.

Extrinsic factors resulting in poor spelling

Some teachers do not think it is necessary to spend time on spelling instruction, considering that most children will learn to spell adequately while engaged in reading and writing activities. However, when systematic spelling instructions is not incorporated into the curriculum there is often a gradual decline in spelling standards, a deterioration which becomes most obvious in the upper end of the junior school.

Although children who have had regular systematic instruction throughout infant and primary school are likely to achieve higher standards in the long run, it is never too late to introduce spelling instruction. Any teacher who feels that she has a classroom of poor spellers should not hesitate to implement a programme of regular spelling instruction.

Many schools have not yet established a spelling policy. This may result in spelling instruction lacking cohesion and direction when children move to a new class. In addition, most teachers are eager to help their pupils achieve a good standard of spelling but are uncertain how to teach it. Establishing a spelling policy and arranging a suitable INSET course is likely to produce the most beneficial outcome.

Teaching spelling

Each individual has a unique balance of cognitive strengths and weaknesses. A child's preferred learning style will play a significant role in determining which type of spelling instruction will be most suitable. Levels of phonological processing, ability to memorize and to recall words and the capacity to make generalizations and formulate hypotheses about how the spelling system works are all important factors in determining the most appropriate teaching for the poor speller.

A child who has good sound skills but poor visual perception and memory skills will respond to different teaching methods than the child with impoverished speech sound skills but an excellent ability to recall letter patterns. Ideally, both approaches should be presented to all children in the classroom, thus enabling individuals to determine which technique is more helpful at that time.

Secondly, the level of a child's spelling skill plays a crucial role in determining which type of spelling instruction is most suitable. The nature of the spelling task alters as children become more competent in their understanding of our spelling system and in their ability to use alternative types of orthographic knowledge when trying to spell unfamiliar words. Hence the type of instruction which is appropriate for a pupil who is still struggling to construct simple regular words will be inappropriate for the child who has excellent alphabetic skills but spells most words using unconventional spellings.

Assessment

Effective remediation necessitates thorough assessment of a child's current spelling and related skills. This should include at the very least:

- A standardized spelling test
- Free-writing produced without any assistance
- Detailed error analysis to provide information about a child's current spelling problems and strategies.

A standardized spelling test provides some indication of the child's levels of achievement in comparison to other children of the same age. Relying upon one's knowledge of the child's position within the class or school is an unreliable measure of a child's level of achievement. Some schools have particularly high standards and a child who appears to be underachieving may, in fact, be performing at an age appropriate level. Similarly, if the spelling standard of a class is relatively low (usually because systematic spelling instruction is not being provided), children who appear to be moderately good spellers may be underachieving substantially.

Since many teachers allow a child to ask for spellings or to use a personal dictionary, teachers are sometimes unaware that a particular child is having unusual difficulty learning spellings or is unable to produce plausible spellings for unfamiliar words. Ten minutes of free-writing is usually sufficient. It is important to note that many children who are able to learn their spellings for spelling tests, then have substantial difficulty recalling the same spellings when engaged in creative writing. This common difficulty is often more pronounced for poor spellers who seem to have inordinate spelling difficulties when they are concentrating on the subject matter of their writing. This discrepancy can be noted during the assessment.

Finally, is the child's writing inordinately slow? If so, the child may eventually be unable to keep up with the rest of the class unless spelling and handwriting skills are improved. Handwriting skills should also be assessed since good spelling is facilitated by good handwriting.

Error analysis is time-consuming but essential. Remediation can only be effective when areas of difficulty are targeted accurately and individualized teaching provided although, of course, children with similar problems can be taught together. The following types of errors are instructive:

(1) *Degree of phonological similarity*: Errors can be analyzed according to their phonological similarity to the word, that is, the extent to which the spelling sounds like the word intended. It is useful to use 3 broad error categories: nonphonetic, partially phonetic and phonetic enabling the teacher to judge mastery of alphabetic skills (none, partial or good).

This preliminary analysis will enable the teacher to identify the developmental stage of the child's spelling. Non-phonetic spelling will indicate that an implicit understanding of correspondence rules has not been attained. The teacher can then examine the child's phonological skills informally (see below). The child may be having difficulty with one or more portions of the encoding process: phoneme segmentation or acquisition and/or application of sound-letter rules.

(2) *Mastery of spelling patterns*: Has the child mastered spelling patterns such as 'sh', 'ar', 'ight', 'ou', 'ee' etc.?

(3) *Morphemes*: plurals and past tense ('-ed'); common suffixes e.g. 'ing', 'ful', 'able/ible' and rules for adding these to words.

(4) *Homophones*: Is the child able to distinguish between words which sound alike but are spelled differently? (Teaching pairs of homophones e.g. 'meat' and 'meet'; 'flower' and 'flour' together can be very confusing. It is preferable to teach each homophone separately grouped with words which have a similar spelling pattern. For example, a child who makes up a silly verse such as 'I eat meat on the seat' is more likely to remember the correct spelling of meat.)

(5) *Lexical knowledge*: Does the child understand that words which have a common word family often share the same basic spelling pattern? e.g. know, known, knowledge; beauty, beautiful; sign, signal.

(6) *Assessment of sound skills*:
(a) Sound Categorization skills can be assessed using the Bradley Test of Auditory Organisation in which the child is asked to listen to a series of 4 words and say which word is different from the other three. There are norms for this test to show whether a child is performing poorly.

(b) Rhyming skills: Can the child recite a nursery rhyme? Ask the child to think of some words which rhyme with 'dog', 'cat', 'tall'.

Children who have excessive difficulty with these two tasks will need extensive instruction in listening to words and identifying phonemes.

(7) Does the child spell primarily by sound and seem to have acquired little word specific knowledge?

Remediation

Poor spelling is not easy to remediate particularly in a busy classroom. However, in many cases the class teacher is the only person who can provide support and instruction. I have tried to concentrate on the most essential requirements of a classroom-based remediation programme.

First and foremost it is essential to separate writing and spelling instruction.

At the commencement of schooling, children who will eventually become poor spellers are not very different from other children. Many are able to express their thoughts clearly and coherently. Many have fertile imaginations and enjoy making up stories. Others find verbal communication difficult, have poor vocabulary skills and have great difficulty organizing their thoughts and selecting appropriate vocabulary. Since spelling is a trivial skill compared to effective communcation every effort must be made to enable an inadequate speller to express thoughts orally and in writing.

No child should be excluded from writing because their spelling is impaired. Children who are unable to invent spellings should be encouraged to dictate stories in a language experience approach. Once children are able to use invented spellings, they should be assisted to write their own stories and helped to decipher their writing before they have forgotten what they wished to write. If help is not immediately at hand, children can dictate their 'writing' into a tape recorder and have their story written out when both the teacher and the child are free. A word processor with a spell check facility can be both an aid and an incentive for such children. Helping a child to communicate successfully using written language is the most constructive way of motivating a child to become an independent writer.

Promoting phonemic awareness

Children whose spelling skill is at a particularly elementary level usually have difficulties with phonological processing and phonemic awareness. Their spelling tends to be nonphonetic or limited to transcription of the first letters. They either refuse to do any free writing or produce work which is often totally incomprehensible. Such spellers often require remediation in phonemic processing skills before spelling instruction can proceed smoothly.

Some nursery teachers, realizing the importance of activities which encourage children to listen to rhyme and alliteration, provide a rich diet of nursery rhymes, encouraging children to make up their own jingles and to listen to the sound similarities in words. Children who are failing to acquire correspondence rules for spelling often require extensive sound categorization activities before and alongside teaching of sound-letter rules.

Using a game such as 'I Spy', teachers of older children can train them to focus on a variety of phonological features in words. Children can be asked to identify objects or classmates whose name begins, ends or contains a particular sound. The game can be extended to focus on groups of speech sounds e.g. 'st' or 'ing'.

Picture games can be bought or constructed using the rules of snap pelmanism or dominoes to encourage children to compare and contrast the sound characteristics of words as an aid to developing phonological processing skills. Versions of pair games based on sound characteristics such as initial or final sound can be made self-corrective by drawing a different pattern on the back of each matching pair of cards. The children can then see if they are correct by checking if the patterns on the back match.

Many schools have adopted developmental writing and spelling programmes for children in the early years. This new trend is an exciting and fruitful teaching approach which is likely to help children learn about the spelling system more successfully than traditional methods permit. However, several dangers accompany this new teaching method. First, teachers need to know how to guide children's learning attempts and not expect such learning to take place without expert direction. Secondly, children who have impaired phonological processing skills will not have adequate skills to be able to benefit from this teaching method. Hence, while linguistically competent children are likely to thrive on this regime, children with linguistic deficits will flounder unless the type of intervention described above is readily available.

Sound-letter rules

The learning of sound-letter rules is essential for children with phonological difficulties who do not extrapolate these rules from their reading and spelling as most normal children do. Bradley and Bryant (1978) have shown that children who were trained to categorize words by sounds and were simultaneously taught the letters which represented the sounds in the words, and made more progress in reading and spelling than children who were not given this specific type of remediation.

Knowledge of sound-letter relationships can be assessed in isolation. The teacher can ask the learner to write the letter which 'makes the sound /t/, /m/, /a/' etc. However, it is necessary to keep an eye on spelling errors as a true measure of a child's working knowledge of sound-letter relationships. Knowing that a particular speech sound can be represented by a certain letter is a far cry from using this knowledge spontaneously when writing. In other words, familiarity with sound-letter relationships does not ensure correct usage in free-writing.

Dictations are an old-fashioned but extremely useful way to allow a child to practise a new correspondence rule and is an important intermediate step for a poor speller. (See dictations in Hornsby and Shear, 1976; Hickey, 1977; Brand, 1988 for examples of structured dictations which *only* ask the child to spell words containing spelling patterns which have already been taught).

Poor spellers tend to forget the spelling patterns they have been taught. They need much revision and over-learning before they can assimilate new sound-letter rules. Fortunately, much of this revision can be accomplished using games and other activities (see Augur, 1989 for some excellent games which can be used in the classroom and sent home as well). It is possible to make pelmanism games or snap games for every sound correspondence rule and letter string introduced. For example, after teaching 'ou' and 'ow', the teacher can write out on cards an even number of words requiring each letter pattern but omitting the critical letters e.g. ' − − t'; 'br_n'; 'h − − se', ' − − l'. The other set of cards will be either 'ou' or 'ow' cards. All the cards are placed face down on the table and each player is allowed to pick up one of each type of card. The player who is able to collect the most pairs is the winner.

A number of teaching programmes intended for children with specific learning difficulties have stressed the value of a highly structured teaching which ensures that a child is taught a small amount of new information at one time, and learns it before additional novel information is introduced. This 'cumulative' type of instruction ensures success and enhances motivation in children who have experienced prolonged failure. Although many teachers would not be able to devote the time necessary to plan an individualized programme for each poor speller in the class, nevertheless the basic principle should be adopted as much as possible.

A structured programme ensures that a child is taught the most basic features of the spelling system first. Most programmes begin by introducing consonants and short vowels gradually. Once all the individual letters have been introduced, consonant blends ('bl', 'st', 'tr', 'spl' etc.) and consonant digraphs ('th', 'sh' etc.) are gradually presented. (See Hornsby and Shear, 1976; Hickey, 1977; Brand, 1988; Miles, 1989 for alternative structured programmes.)

Many poor spellers have great difficulty identifying short vowels such as the /a/ in cat, the /i/ in pin, and the /e/ in /pen/. When asked if 'pin' and 'pen' are the same words, they generally have no trouble recognizing that the words are different but they flounder when trying to identify which short vowel to use when spelling. The child should select a clue word which can be referred to if there is any uncertainty about the sound of a vowel. Traditionally, the clue words for the short vowel sounds have been apple /a/, elephant /e/, igloo /i/, orange /o/ and umbrella /u/ but children may well prefer to select their own words. Make sure that the word is imageable so that the child can draw the clue word and be able to identify it as necessary. It is best to teach one new vowel at a time, gradually introducing another vowel when the first has been adequately learned. These children may need many weeks of exercises and games requiring vowel discrimination and the selection of the correct vowel before other correspondences are taught.

At a substantially more advanced stage the alternative representations of long vowels and vowel digraphs are taught, generally culminating in the teaching spelling choices in which the learner is actively helped to work out the relative probabilities of the alternative spelling patterns which can be used to represent one sound. (See Table 7.1).

Table 7.1

Spelling choices for the long /a/ phoneme.

Spelling pattern	Clue word	Position in word
a–e	name	middle
ai	rain	beginning/middle
ay	day	end
ey	gr	end
ei	reign	middle

Use word lists which are structured according to basic orthographic patterns and phonological patterns as for example:

bin	bread	house
kin	head	louse
thin		mouse
pin		
win		

or for older children use morphemic families in which spelling patterns are based on units of meaning:

photo graph
photo graph*er*
photo graph*y*

photo
photo synthesis

*graph*ic
geo*graph*y

Learning whole words

It is vital for teachers to provide clear directives about alternative methods for learning whole words so that poor spellers are able to learn the words which they are eager to learn to spell. It is particularly unproductive and frustrating to give poor spellers a list of words to learn without any further instructions. Three different techniques are presented here. The teacher can help learners find the one that is most effective and encourage them to use that technique whenever they need to learn whole words. Most poor spellers require the kinaesthetic feedback which is provided by the Simultaneous Oral Spelling and the Fernald procedures. As learning whole words becomes more proficient, the simpler 'Look, Cover, Write, Check' procedure may suffice.

I. Bradley's Simultaneous Oral Spelling (1981)

This routine is multi-sensory, requiring the child to *listen* to the word, to *say* the word, hearing and feeling how the word is formed in the mouth, and finally to *write* the word while feeling the motor movements which are needed to write the word. In this way the learner is encouraged to use all the senses when memorizing the word so that faulty sensory channels may be reinforced by more efficient channels (Hickey, 1987). For clarity I have given instructions in note form.

(1) The teacher constructs the word using plastic letters or writing the word out clearly on a card. Then the teacher says the word.

(2) The learner repeats the word.

(3) The learner writes the word in cursive script *saying the name of each letter as it is written.*

(4) The word is pronounced again.

(5) The learner confirms that the word has been written correctly.

(6) The learner repeats steps 2–5 until the word has been written accurately on at least 3 successive occasions.

(7) The learner then covers the word and writes it from memory naming each letter as it is written. After each attempt the child checks to ensure that the word has been written correctly.

II. Fernald (1943)

Fernald used this method to teach nonreaders and spellers words which they particularly wished to learn. She believed that tracing the word enabled beginners to recall the spellings more accurately than just looking at the words. Note that she insists that the syllables should be pronounced as they are written and not the letter names as in Simultaneous Oral Spelling.

(1) Teacher pronounces the word, and writes it in large letters on a card.

(2) Child repeats it.

(3) Child traces the word with a finger and pronounces each syllable while tracing it.

(4) After tracing it several times, the learner writes it from memory.

(5) Child checks the spelling.

(6) If the spelling was correct, it is written from memory again, if not – resume tracing until successful and then continue with step 5.

III. Look, Cover, Write, Check

This procedure has been advanced by Peters (1985) and Cripps for over a decade and has proved a valuable technique for normal spellers although it is less successful for poor spellers whose visual memory and orthographic knowledge is elementary.

(1) The teacher writes the word.

(2) LOOK. The child studies the word in order to learn the spelling.

Initially it may be helpful to give hints about the best way to learn the word.

(3) COVER. When the child feels confident that the word has been learned, the child covers the word so it is no longer visible.

(4) WRITE. The child writes the word from memory.

(5) CHECK. The child then checks the spelling against the original version to see if the spelling was accurate.

(6) If it is correct, the cover, write, check procedure should be repeated until the spelling can be reproduced at least 3 times. If the word is incorrect, then the learner should resume step 2 until the spelling can be written from memory without looking.

Although the methods have distinctive chracteristics, they also have many similarities. In practice I have found that many teachers amalgamate features of each technique. For example, it is possible to have the learner name the letters when using the 'Look, Cover, Write, Check' routine. This addition focuses the child's attention on the individual letters as well as providing auditory and oral-kinaesthetic feedback.

The 'check' portion of all these techniques is found extremely difficult by most poor spellers. The teacher should ensure that each letter is checked systematically and not just glanced at. Many poor spellers tend to identify words using partial cues only (Frith, 1984) and this cursory method of word identification precludes accurate proofreading.

Helping poor spellers requires thorough assessment and individualised teaching which aims to ensure success by providing instruction at the appropriate level for each child. Using a battery of games to reinforce each sound pattern or spelling pattern as it is introduced can provide the additional revision which poor spellers invariably need. Above all, poor spellers need classroom teachers who understand that learning to spell can be extremely difficult for some. In treating the problem with understanding and sympathy alongside structured individualised teaching the prognosis for such children should improve.

CHAPTER 8

Perceptual Motor Problems Related to Literacy

Barbara Noad

The incidence of perceptual motor difficulties

In my experience as a Learning Support Teacher, I have found that one of the aspects of behaviour exhibited by children with specific learning difficulties, which concerns both parents and teachers, is the inability of some children to perform well in activities which require accurate, fluent and appropriate use of the body. It is problems with handwriting and other fine motor skills which tend to be mentioned most frequently, but other behaviours such as poor gross motor co-ordination, fidgeting, lack of concentration, self-help difficulties such as dressing and a general awkwardness are reported.

Further discussion with parents often reveals a history of delay in achieving developmental milestones – sitting, walking, running. There may have been difficulties in learning to dress or use a knife and fork and later acquiring more complex perceptual motor skills, such as riding a bicycle or learning to swim. However, although some clumsy children have literacy problems, others do not. Conversely, there are children diagnosed as having specific learning disorders, who have no problems of this type.

Research which has been carried out into the causes of literacy difficulties has included references to this aspect of learning dysfunction. Orton (1937), Critchley (1964), Naidoo (1972) and Taylor (1982) all describe aspects of body competence problems in a proportion of the children that they studied.

Sensory motor organisation problems

Whatever the cause of the clumsiness, the clumsy child who also has a literacy problem is at an even greater disadvantage when compared with his peers.

Naidoo (1972) concluded that learning to read, write and spell depends on the ability of the child to form automatic and permanent associations between what they see, hear, say and write and that failure lies in the inability to do this. A number of the speakers at the Dyslexia World Congress (1989) indicated that the problem encountered by these children is primarily one of organisation. That is, organisation of sensory stimuli to elicit an automatic response whether in reading, writing or other related skills.

Tansley (1967) and Hickey (1977) list four sensory input systems which are of particular importance in the development of literacy skills. Both authors list the visual sensory system and the auditory sensory system, then name two which have a direct motor component; Hickey names the tactile kinaesthetic system and the oral kinaesthetic system, and Tansley mentions the kinesthetic motor channel and the tactile cutaneous channel.

They maintain that it is the interaction and organisation of these sensory systems within the brain – sensory integration – which is vital for a correct automatic response. A defect in one or more systems will change the overall integration process. Sensory integration results in perception and concept formation, which are essential for effective interaction with the environment, leading to learning.

Children with an inability to organise their bodies may be affected intellectually, socially and emotionally. Their lives tend to be disorganised, not just in movement but in other aspects. They seem to live in a muddle, never knowing where they should be or when. Often their general appearance is untidy and they are forever losing something. Clumsy children frequently complain that 'they cannot make their hands do what their eyes see' (Cruikshank, 1973).

As a result the child who cannot control movements appropriately develops a poor self image (Cratty, 1967). When asked 'What is the effect of dyslexia?' an intelligent, articulate twenty-one year old woman stated, 'Mainly, it is terribly destructive to your self confidence, because reading and writing are supposedly so easy!' This equally well applies to the clumsy child – fastening buttons, catching a ball, writing neatly, are supposedly so easy.

Children develop self concept by comparing performance with that

90

of their peers, and through the approval or disapproval of the adults with whom they are in contact. A child who moves with ease and performs motor tasks skilfully has a positive self image, high peer group esteem and adult approval.

Bedford and Alston (1987) describe the clumsy child as 'lacking in grace'. It is the quality of movement, rather than a lack of it, which is the problem. The performance level may not be poor, but it is the way a child perceives performance, that either builds or destroys self confidence.

Rejection by peers can lead to social isolation. Nobody wants a 'butter fingers' on their team. Poor handling of utensils at meal times can incur adult disapproval. Slowness in dressing following a P.E. lesson may irritate a teacher. Eventually the children will consider themselves inferior and refuse to try activities. They then become labelled as lazy or poorly motivated.

These children need help not only to feel competent in literacy skills, but also in the ability to use the body effectively.

The body – skills and concepts

Before considering any form of intervention and possible remediation it is important to consider what the prime functions of the body are and the skills and concepts the child needs to acquire in order to use it confidently.

The body cannot be regarded in isolation. The mind and body must be in harmony as they affect and reflect each other. If the mind is under stress, this will affect the body; for instance a child who has the combined difficulties described above, is under stress all day, both at school and at home. As a result there is an increase in clumsiness. The child is caught in a cycle of difficulty from which the only channels of escape may be: opting out, by becoming the class clown, or indulging in disruptive, inappropriate behaviour.

Possibly one of the best descriptions of the body, is that defined in the philosophy of Psychomotor Therapy (Burr, 1988). The body is:

- a pivot
- a means of contact
- a means of controlling the environment
- a medium of the mind.

It is a pivot – a reference point for all experience. It is a connection with and a means of controlling the environment which enable learning to take place. It is a medium for expression, through which emotions are transmitted and communication is made with others.

In the development of higher learning skills such as literacy, numeracy, art or music, the role of the body is less apparent than that of vision or hearing.

Laszlo and Bairstow (1985) maintain that all overt behaviour is expressed through movement, whether as part of social intercourse or part of interaction with the environment. In order to do these successfully the child must acquire certain skills and concepts.

The skills can be divided into two groups –

- perceptual motor skills
- non-verbal communication skills.

Perceptual motor skills

(1) *Balance.* As children move from the prone or supine position (apedal) to the upright position (bipedal) they need to be able to balance – to maintain a posture – in order to carry out further interaction with their environment. During this process they develop laterality, an awareness of the two sides of the body and their differences; directionality, the ability to project this knowledge from themselves into the space around them; and symmetry, the ability to use both sides of the body in unison.

In order to achieve balance a child needs posture, which is the basic movement pattern out of which all other movement patterns must develop. It is a positive neuromuscular act which maintains the body in its correct position with reference to its centre of gravity. This act is reflexive and overrides all other conscious or unconscious movement. If a child is walking along a garden wall, as soon as s/he begins to wobble and lose balance, the body reacts to bring her/him back to the position which is necessary to maintain balance. Kephart (1960) states that movement not in accord with basic posture cannot be performed. All movement, therefore all overt behaviour, must develop out of the body's ability to maintain posture.

The easiest posture to maintain is lying flat on a hard surface. One of the most difficult postures is standing on one leg. The body has to achieve equilibrium, whether it is to maintain Static balance, when it wishes to remain still, or Dynamic balance, when it is moving. The degree of movement involved in the latter ranges from hardly perceptible to very obvious.

Background postures are those which are necessary to fixate and maintain the body or parts of the body, in balance, in order to allow other parts of the body to carry out specific tasks, for instance fixation of the shoulder girdle to enable the child to write with ease. Good background postures are necessary before any accurate fine movement can take place.

When the child has integrated balance skills at an unconscious level in the brain, and equilibrium can be achieved automatically, s/he is then able to receive and integrate the information which is necessary to acquire symbolic skills, reading etc.

(2) *Motor Planning*. A child develops the capacity to plan new movements based on the body scheme (Ayres, 1972). This ability to motor plan should be unconscious. The child who is constantly turning attention from an activity, to how to perform that activity, does not interact easily with the environment and increase knowledge. '... if the brain develops the capacity to perceive, remember and motor plan, the ability can then be applied to the mastery of all academic and other tasks, regardless of specific content.' (Ayres, 1972).

Non-verbal communication skills

There are two areas of non-verbal communication skills:

(1) *Body Gesture*, the skill to communicate non-verbally, is learned by observation of peers and adults. For most children, early learning takes place at home. Consider a mother shaking her head to indicate that she wants an inappropriate behaviour to cease or opening her arms wide for a child to run into when it is distressed.

A large amount of classroom control is non-verbal in nature. In order to interpret and learn appropriate gestures the child must have a good body image and awareness of movement.

(2) *Facial Expression* is linked with body gesture. The interpretation of expressions of joy, anger, sorrow and other emotions are learned by observation. The ability to repeat them as required needs a knowledge of the facial parts and how to move them.

As I mentioned above, the development of motor planning and non-verbal communication skills is based on the concept of body image (knowledge of body parts) and body scheme (awareness of movement potential). In order to acquire these concepts, information from a number of sensory input channels needs to be integrated into the central nervous system (C.N.S.). This information is received simultaneously through all channels and integrated to form the whole. These channels are:

- *Visual* – information which is received through the eyes.
- *Auditory* – information which is received through the ears.
- *Tactile* – information which is received from the skin. This is the earliest sensory channel to be used by the child. Sensations received from the skin not only help the child to build a body image but also allow the child to gain knowledge about the properties of objects and his/her relationship to them – for instance a hot cup, a slippery floor or a sharp knife.
- *Proprioceptive* – information which is received from the muscles, joints and bones. Much of this input is unconscious and is associated with reflexes and automatic responses. However, proprioceptive sensations can come to conscious awareness when attention is deliberately focused on them. This occurs when learning a new sequence of motor patterns such as those necessary to drive a car. Proprioceptive input also monitors the amount of pressure or effort needed to carry out a task.
- *Kinaesthetic* – information received from the joints which tells the child where the various parts of the body are in space and which movements they are making. It enables a child to hit a ball without looking to see where the bat is in space, or kick a ball without visually checking his foot position.
- *Vestibular* – information from the inner ear. It enables the child to detect motion and gravity. It also enables them to know whether any given sensory input is associated with the body or is a function of the environment. Is s/he moving in the room or is the room moving around them?

As the child's body is the point of reference, around which s/he orders the world, it is essential that s/he establishes a good body image and scheme. S/he must be able to label the parts of the body – hand, nose, chin etc. and the movements which it is capable of making – walking, running, sitting, climbing, if s/he is to become competent when interacting with the environment.

Laszlo and Bairstow (1985) maintain that it is the kinaesthetic sensory system which is the most important in acquiring good perceptual motor skills. The kinaesthetic sense stores the memory for movements, and monitors such movement, correcting errors via

94

feedback to the Central Nervous System. A child who has a poorly developed kinaesthetic sensory system will not easily remember movement patterns. As a consequence s/he will not be able to repeat them in a consistent way. The physical ability is adequate for the performance, the organisation is not. Each time the task is performed, it is always the first time. Therefore learning to write is a very difficult task. Although the proportion of children who are dyskinaesthetic is small, this problem should be borne in mind as a possible dysfunction, in children with severe handwriting problems.

Changes take place in the nervous system when a new motor pattern is learned. These changes are permanent, although they may diminish, if the skill is not used over a period of time. A swimmer will soon swim again even if they have not been in a pool for a number of years. Incorrect motor patterns are also retained and are very difficult to correct. This has implications for the initial teaching of handwriting. D. Montgomery at a conference on handwriting used the phrase 'Practice makes permanent'. Practice makes perfect only when the basic movement is correct.

Intervention and remediation

General perceptual motor skills

Research and experience have shown that there is no cure for clumsiness. However, intervention programmes can give the child more confidence, by improving the ability to perform tasks, which leads to changes in self concept and motivation. They can also help in the development of coping strategies.

Focusing on the problem raises awareness in the adults involved, at the same time giving them the knowledge needed to support the child in a constructive way.

Learning is developmental. It is a spiral process which incorporates new experiences into previous memories, modifying them in the process to produce a new response (Ayres, 1972).

There are many books and articles which describe methods of assessment and remedial programmes, based on a number of disparate theories. Some are designed for the teacher, whilst others are suitable for therapists and those with special training. (A selection of these will be given at the end of the chapter.) Many recommend improving various skill areas such as ball throwing and catching. Few describe how to begin, and a method of developing a hierarchy which will refine and improve skills.

The teacher is aware by observation which behaviours are causing problems for the child. Regardless of the cause (excluding conditions which produce gross motor defects), she can begin to devise intervention programmes by analysing the basic underlying skills necessary to perform a task such as ball catching or ball throwing.

In order to be good at the former activity a child needs to be able to judge:

- the direction from which the ball is coming (directionality)
- the speed at which it is travelling (velocity)
- the point of intervention.

Next, the teacher must consider the most appropriate way for the child to learn these skills without constant failure and frustration.

One method which I have found successful, is to seat the child or children on the floor, opposite the teacher, with their feet apart. The teacher rolls a large, soft ball towards the child saying 'catch' when she knows it is in the correct position for intervention. She remains in total control of the situation and can vary the speed and direction of the ball and there is minimal risk of failure for the child. By altering the distance, size and weight of the ball, the floor surface, or asking the children to catch with their feet, the task can be made more demanding. Once the child is consistently competent in this position, catching can be introduced in a sitting, then kneeling and eventually standing position.

In order to be competent in the latter activity, throwing, the child must be able to judge:

- the distance and direction which the ball has to travel.
- the amount of force required to place the ball at the point of intervention.

These skills apply whether the ball is to be caught, hit or placed in a container.

Again, a child needs to succeed quickly without a high level of frustration. As beanbags are much easier to control than balls they should be used in the initial stages. Stand the children around a large hoop (about a meter away from it), each with a supply of beanbags. Then ask them to see how many they can throw into it. By using a smaller hoop or moving the children further back, the task becomes more difficult and the skill level increases. Eventually the beanbags can be replaced by small sponge balls which are thrown into a large box or large sponge balls thrown to a partner.

Similar analysis of motor tasks will enable a teacher to devise suitable programmes using her own experience and advisory books. Each lesson should include activities involving various aspects of body skills and concepts – balance, body image, awareness of muscle tone, motor planning and spatial orientation, using activities such as obstacle races, ball games, 'Simon Says' and many others.

Handwriting

The introduction of the National Curriculum has focused attention on the skill of handwriting, by making it one of the Attainment Targets. This has generated a new interest in teaching methods. The consensus of opinion at a recent conference given by the Handwriting Interest Group, was that handwriting is a precise and complex skill which must be very carefully taught. As I pointed out earlier in the chapter, incorrect movement patterns are quickly established and difficult to correct. A child does not know instinctively which way round to form letters nor the correct methods of joining them together. This is particularly true for a child with specific learning difficulties who also experiences motor co-ordination problems. It is beneficial to all children if they are taught a running or cursive script from the reception class. For children with difficulties, it could be said that this is essential if they are to achieve a fluent, legible style of writing.

A number of books, articles and resources are available for the teacher to refer to, when attempting to remediate handwriting. M. D. Klein (1982, 1987) in her books *Pre-writing Skills* and *Pre-scissor Skills*, gives clear descriptions of the skills needed, before a child can begin to write or use scissors successfully. These include the ability to balance and sustain background postures, the ability to use the hands together in lead-assistor fashion, the ability to coordinate hand/eye movements. Such skills are relevant to the older child as well as the beginner. It is, however, rarely possible for the teacher to take the child into the gym to improve the basic skill areas, before attempting remediation, and research has indicated that isolated skill training is often not effective in achieving overall improvement.

The retraining of correct movement patterns, using the non-writing hand to assist, is successful with some children, beginning on a blackboard initially, before transferring to the horizontal writing position. Once the pattern has been experienced and practised, a check can be made to determine whether the motor pattern is being established, by asking the child to repeat the pattern with closed eyes.

Jarman (1987) advocates daily tuition and practice when developing handwriting skills. This is even more important for the child with perceptual motor problems. Boring repetition should be avoided and self assessment of progress encouraged.

Research in 1980 by Briggs showed that handwriting difficulties can influence grades in 16+ examinations. Therefore remediation is important.

Conclusion

Although a child may have perceptual motor difficulties, these need not become a major problem, if they are treated with understanding and suitable support given.

Early recognition is important before defensive behaviours can become established. Prior to the Specific Learning Disability becoming apparent, a teacher may become aware of immaturity in the gross and fine motor development of a child. Intervention at this stage may determine whether this is due to a developmental lag, possibly caused by a lack of experience or a more specific perceptual motor difficulty. If the problem appears severe and is causing the child high levels of frustration then consultation with the parents and the School Medical Officer is advisable. When children are diagnosed as having specific learning disabilities, the Perceptual Motor aspect of their overall development should be checked, and suitable activities included in their remedial programme if necessary. Although the class teacher may not be responsible for the literacy aspects of the programme, the motor aspect could be part of the overall class organisation.

References

Perceptual motor programmes

Deiner, P. L. (1983). *Resources for Teaching Young Children with Special Needs*. London: Harcourt Brace Jovanovich.

Gilroy, P. J. (1984). *Kids in Action – Devloping Body Awareness in Young Children*. Arizona: Communication Skill Builders Inc.

Gilroy, P. J. (1985). *Kids in Motion – An Early Childhood Movement Education Program*. Arizona: Communication Skill Builders Inc.

98

Gordon, N. and McKinlay, I. (1980). *Helping Clumsy Children*. Churchill Livingstone.

Nash-Wortham, M. (1987). 'The clumsy, poorly co-ordinated child with associated reading and writing difficulties'. *Support for Learning*, Vol. 2.4:36:40.

Russell, J. P. (1988). *Graded Activities for Children with Motor Difficulties*. Cambridge: Cambridge University Press.

Tansley, A. E. (1990). *Motor Education*. Exeter: Arnold Wheaton.

Taylor, K. J. (1982). *Physical Awkwardness and Reading Disability*. M.Sc. dissertation, University of Alberta, Canada.

Wallace, J. (1988). 'The Clumsy Child – classroom implications'. *Gnosis*, **12**, 31–37.

Handwriting resources – remedial

Alston, J. and Taylor, J. (1988). *The Handwriting File*. L.D.A., Duke St., Wisbech, Cambs.

Pickard, P. (1986). *Handwriting – A Second Chance*. Wisbech: L.D.A.

Sassoon, R. *Helping Your Handwriting*. Teacher and Pupil Books. Exeter: Arnold Wheaton.

Stott, D. H., Moyes, A. and Henderson, S. *Diagnosis and Remediation of Handwriting Problems*. Cardiff: Drake Education.

Handwriting resources – initial training

Cripps, C. R. and Cox, R. (1984). *Joining the A.B.C.* Wisbech: L.D.A.

Cripps, C. (1985). *A Hand for Spelling – Books 1–4*. Wisbech: L.D.A.

Jarman, C. (1987). *The Development of Handwriting Skills and Workbooks* Oxford: Basil Blackwell.

Sassoon, R. (1983). *A Practical Guide to Children's Handwriting*. London Thames and Hudson.

Sassoon, R. (1990). *Handwriting: The Way to Teach it*. Cheltenham: Stanley Thornes.

Sassoon, R. (1990). *Handwriting: A New Perspective*. Cheltenham: Stanley Thornes.

Smith, P. and Inglis, A. *New Nelson Handwriting*. Walton-on-Thames Nelson.

Further reading

Alston, J. and Taylor, J. (1987). *Handwriting, Theory, Research and Practice* London: Croom Helm.

Alston, J. (1987, 1988, 1989). *Handwriting Review*. Dept of Special Education, Crewe and Alsager College of Higher Education, CR1 1DU.

CHAPTER 9

Authors not Victims:
Writing with Word Processors

Ann Baldwin

Writing is both a process and a product. The English National Curriculum divides the profile component into three Attainment Targets:

Attainment Target 3:	A growing ability to construct and convey meaning in written language, matching style to audience and purpose.
Attainment Target 4:	Spelling (Levels 1–4 only)
Attainment Target 5:	Handwriting (Levels 1–4 only)
or Attainment Target 4/5:	Presentation (Levels 5–7)

The communication of ideas in writing poses problems for most children, let alone those with learning difficulties. Anything which facilitates 'getting thoughts onto paper' will be a welcome addition to any classroom. The word processor can do this, but not entirely without planned intervention from the teacher. It is naive to believe that it is a magic tool which produces perfect composition without really trying.

What is near magical is the liberating effect that the word processor can have on children with handwriting difficulties: text emerges from the printer in a form which everyone can read, including the writer! All i's are dotted, t's crossed, letters are uniform in size and face in the right direction, lines are horizontal, and words always fit onto the page. There are no smudges, no crossings-out, no ugly holes in the paper made by desperate attempts to eliminate things unpleasant. Th first time a child sees his or her work in print s/he can hardly believe it 'Did I write that?' For the child with learning difficulties this can be a important step towards recognising that writing is more than th laboured production of strings of untameable letters.

In order to reach Level 2 of Attainment Target 4 a child must be ab to 'Produce letters that are recognisably formed and properly oriente and that have clear ascenders and descenders where necessary.' S/h won't learn that using a computer. However, the Cox Report contair the following caveat:

> Some pupils with physical disabilities may require the writir attainment targets to be modified. For, example, the handwritir target, which applies up to Level 4, and the presentation target, whic applies from Level 5 to 7, might be inappropriate. Such pupils shoul be enabled to produce their written work on a word processor c concept keyboard.

The value of a word processor lies in its capacity for allowing childre to write fluently in closer synchronisation with their own thoughts tha is possible using a pen or pencil. You have only to observe the vast ga between a pupil's oral story-telling ability and his or her attempts a story-telling to appreciate the obstacle that poor motor control ca pose in the process of composition.

> Darren, a bright chatty 8 year-old with a passion for motor-bikes, ha entertained the class with his tale of a cross-country rally.

> 'There was mud flying and wheels slipping. One man fell off an' his su was all slimy. The engines were just screaming when they bust over th hill an' . . . '

> His face shone with excitement. Taking advantage of his obviou interest in the subject, his teacher suggested that he wrote it up for th wall. Two days later he slipped a screwed up piece of paper under he nose and skulked off. It read: 'I like moter-biks'. When she asked hir why he hadn't written more, he said flatly, 'My pencil broke.'

> In other words, the physical effort of writing was too great.

Of course, there is a physical effort involved in using a word processc too. The keyboard must be mastered, though not in the sense that touch-typist masters it, using all ten fingers. Not everybody know that. Recently I heard a computer-shy teacher say 'I couldn't teach m class to use the computer because I can't type.'

There are two things wrong with that remark. Firstly, if you ca read the characters on the keys, you can type, albeit with one finger. Secondly, children can teach themselves to use the keyboard – and usually do. I'm a great believer in allowing pupils a reasonable 'hands-on' period as a first step to learning to use the word processor. Let them make their own mistakes for a while. In fact, encourage them to get used to seeing mistakes appear on the screen. One of the worst blocks to composition is fear of imperfections. The word processor allows the child to write inaccurate nonsense and turn it into accurate sense painlessly.

S/he will soon learn that pressing a key for too long will cause the character to recur alarmingly; that words will automatically 'wrap around' when they reach the end of the line; that without pressing a second key only lower-case characters will be produced. Understanding the function of the cursor is best learned in context, too.

The teacher will gauge the appropriate moment to tell individuals how to use the Delete key, how to press the Shift key to produce capital letters. She will encourage attempts at inserting new text using the directional keys to move the cursor backwards or forwards, up or down. Text embellishments like emboldening, underlining, tabulation, centring and double spacing can come later. For the time being it is better to keep it simple so that results are achieved quickly, especially bearing in mind the short concentration span of some children with learning difficulties. However, teaching how to Save and Print documents will prevent the demotivating disappointment of losing precious text and ensure that it can be revised or completed at a later date.

The QUINKEY Keyboard

There are alternatives to the QWERTY keyboard which teachers of children with special needs might like to consider. After all, the layout of the standard keyboard deliberately made it impossible for typists to type too fast in case they jammed the keys on the early Remingtons. QUINKEY is a six-key board designed to work with the BBC computer. The six keys can be used in various combinations to produce the full range of characters. Up to four boards can be used simultaneously with one computer enabling computers to be employed more intensively in the classroom. Surveys have shown that after an hour's use children using the QUINKEY keyboard can type more quickly than those using the QWERTY.

The CONCEPT Keyboard

A CONCEPT keyboard is a flat rectangular grid which can be plugged into the computer's underside. It consists of 128 pressure-sensitive sections, each of which can be programmed by the teacher to produce several lines of text, or a phrase, a whole word, a single character, a picture or a symbol in any configuration she chooses. An attractive overlay is then placed on the board, indicating what will appear on the screen when each area is pressed. For children with very poor motor control quite large areas can be allocated to each symbol or piece of text, reducing the likelihood of hitting the wrong rectangle.

The advantage of this alternative system is that the teacher creates the content to suit the child's ability and interest.

> Seven-year-old Sarah is physically disabled and unable to hold a pencil. She had been watching frog-spawn turn into tadpoles and wanted to write about it like the other children in her class. Sometimes her teacher would make a transcript of what she said in her own handwriting, but this didn't make Sarah 'feel like a writer'. The teacher decided to design an overlay for the Concept Keyboard containing most of the words and phrases Sarah wanted. Used in conjunction with PROMPT/WRITER, minor editing could be done afterwards by the teacher.

See Figure 9.1 for an example of a Concept Keyboard overlay.

The 'language-experience' approach of the Concept Keyboard has many of the advantages of the *Breakthrough to Literacy* scheme whose aim was to turn speakers into writers. Slow writers so often end up with a collection of unfinished texts. A further advantage of using CONCEPT rather than QWERTY is that it speeds up the writing process, giving children a greater sense of achievement.

Children with spelling difficulties

> Pupils with specific learning difficulties (dyslexia)...may however have particular difficulty with the attainment targets concerned with 'secretarial' skills, and in this respect they may benefit particularly from using word processors, including spelling checkers. (12.10)

Imaginative children with poor spelling skills are often frustrated in their attempts to compose elaborate text. Their minds may be fertile with words like 'transparent', 'glistening', and 'terrifying' which never make it onto the page for fear they end up unintelligible to the reader. Substitutes such as 'clear', 'shiny' and 'bad' strip the narrative

I	we	you	they	me	saw	pond	
am	are		them		hopped	frog	
was	of	were		suddenly	hopping	spawn	
out	the		fast	quickly	waited	tadpoles	
in	up	today	black		swimming	water	←
by	down	then	big	Spring	wiggling	plants	rubber
on			small		watched	jelly	~~~ new line
under	lots		fat		eat	tail	

Figure 9.1 The Concept Keyboard – A typical overlay

of its atmosphere. The result may be a series of bald statements. The Concept Keyboard increases the child's chances of producing readable text. An overlay on the Concept Keyboard containing dozens of descriptive words generated by the child can be used in conjunction with the QWERTY keyboard. This creates greater freedom for composition than would be possible with the Concept Keyboard alone. Lists of words can be drawn up by a small group of children who are working together on a particular topic. This is especially useful for projects involving the use of technical vocabulary whose spelling may be unfamiliar. The selection of the words themselves can be the subject of valuable group discussion about language (cf. Level 5 of Attainment Target 1 in the National Curriculum in English: 'Talk about variations in vocabulary . . . e.g. specialist terms).'

Some 'content' programs, such as LOST FROG, which were written for the QWERTY keyboard can now be accessed via the Concept Keyboard, using a piece of softwear called CONCEPT produced by MESU's Special Needs Software Centre. This overcomes the problem poor spellers often have of finding that their commands are rejected because the computer 'does not understand' them. All the words they need to play the game are spelled for them.

To attain Level 3 of Attainment Target 4 in the English National Curriculum children must 'In revising and re-drafting their writing begin to check the accuracy of their spelling.' Very poor spellers may go through the motions of re-reading their work but will rarely spot their mistakes. This is where the computer spell checker can be such boon. Many word processing programs have this facility. Pressing simple combination of function keys after typing a text will highlight misspelt words. Some programs will even suggest alternative spellings. This can be helpful in directing the child to the appropriate part of the dictionary. S/he can then check the word against its definition in order to find out if it is the one s/he wants. Children can build up wordbank of words they frequently misspell. Screen highlighting is so much more friendly than a teacher's pencil-line under an incorrect spelling.

Presentation

It would be wrong to claim that print always looks better than handwriting. Some children take enormous pride in forming the letters and are constantly experimenting with different styles. The decorate capital letters in the manner of mediaeval scribes. Hand writing for them is a craft. Nevertheless there is somethin authoritative about a text which appears in print. Children associate print with real books and magazines and newspapers. When they first see their own words in print they feel as if they have achieved publication.

A Desk-Top Publishing program makes it possible for children to manipulate print in ways which would otherwise only be achievable with a simpler word processing package using 'cut-and-paste' and photocopying after printout. Even a relatively unsophisticated program like FRONT PAGE EXTRA enables cutting, pasting and newspaper formatting to be carried out on-screen. Some programs allow graphics to be inserted into the text so that the final printout looks exactly like a real newspaper. Reluctant writers find this kind of final product extremely motivating. Often the space for the text itself is limited so that it is possible for the struggling writer to produce quite short articles which fill a whole page. Groups of children can easily publish a whole newspaper which can be distributed to other classes or parents. This gives a real purpose to their writing which is sometimes missing in the daily diary writing activity once so popular in primary classrooms.

Many word processing packages offer a range of print fonts (i.e. typefaces) including pica, elite, italic, Roman, even gothic! Programs which produce oversize print are particularly helpful to the slow reader. Arts and language are truly combined in a program like PENDOWN which allows children to design their own fonts. Before we dismiss this as gimmickry it is worth noting the value of this in, say, poetry writing. It is possible to convey the mood of the words in the design of the font: psychedelic, stripy characters for rap, delicate curly characters for a love poem.

SIGNWRITER does just what it says, enabling teachers to produce labels and signs of a high quality. Anything which makes the classroom environment more stimulating is likely to have its positive effect on children with learning difficulties, especially where it facilitates the acquisition of language in context.

Composing on the computer

So much for the pretty products. How can word processors facilitate composition – the process of writing – for children with learning difficulties?

To discuss this we first need to consider what is involved in the process of composing. See Figure 9.2.

MODEL OF COMPOSITION PROCESS

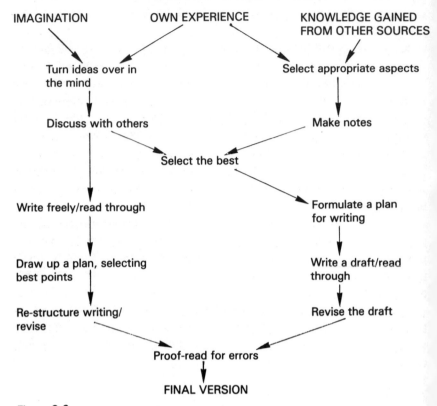

Figure 9.2

In this model, the right-hand route is the traditional one, most appropriate for more formal transactional writing – a discussion essay, a set of instructions, a news report. Its emphasis is upon structure – a beginning, a middle and an end. The requirement for clear, sustained thinking is what causes the less able pupil to come unstuck. Little wonder that s/he resorts to copying from source materials – surely they *must* be right? Such pupils do not regard themselves as authors, but rather as victims of the text which threaten to tie them in knots.

The left-hand route is less restrictive, and is appropriate for creative or personal writing – diaries, descriptions, poems, personal letters. Structure anyway comes more naturally in a diary since events are related in chronological order. And who but the writer can say what should be the structure or content of poetry?

Although the transactional route is the more problematical of the two in the early stages of composition, the word processor will most fruitfully be introduced to special needs pupils during the expressive writing process. For it is here that they can learn to reflect at the level of the sentence and the word rather than the more unwieldy paragraph.

The English National Curriculum requires that children should know 'when and how to plan, draft, re-draft, revise and proof-read their work' (17.15). This must be viewed alongside the statement that 'teacher assessment should take account of the way pupils tackle writing tasks – that is, it should be sensitive to the writing process as well as to the finished product.' It further suggests that pupils 'should play an active part in assessing their own progress through discussion with those who read their writing – their peers, teachers or other adults.' (17.18).

It is no earthly use sitting a child in front of a word processor and expecting him or her to 'draft, re-draft, revise' without help. All s/he will do is proof-read for technical errors and correct them. A major advantage of the computer screen over the page is that it is usually bigger and it is vertical, making the text accessible to several children at the same time. They can read aloud and respond to each other's work as it appears on the screen. They can also write collaboratively.

The following conversation took place between three 8-year-olds engaged in descriptive writing about Spring.

LARA (reading from the screen)
> '. . . and then the butterfly landed on a pink flower and then it landed on a blue flower . . . ' Phew! And then, and then – you keep saying 'and then.'

LEROY (at the keyboard)
> I just seem to keep writing it. I'll take it out later. Now I'll make him land on a pink – no, I've already said that – (typing) 'a yellow flower'.

KIRSTY Him! Is it a 'him'?

LARA What *kind* of a yellow flower? I want to know what kind. You know – a buttercup or a –

LEROY A primrose – a pale primrose! (inserting the additional text). I'm changing it to a beautiful pale yellow primrose.

Lara's initial remark is critical of the fact that Leroy is writing like he talks, but this is seen by Leroy as no more than a mechanical problem. He'll attend to it later. He is well aware that he is 'thinking on screen', but screen-writing is impermanent and gives rise to none of the inhibitions associated with putting pen to paper. However, Lara's second comment – a question – is the result of genuine curiosity about what only the writer can reveal – 'What kind of flower is it?' Leroy's response is immediate and excited. His idea grows as he talks, as he types. Where the word processor is so important is in the freedom it gives him to manipulate text without mutilating it. He is the author, not the victim: 'I'll *make* him land . . .'

Providing opportunities for pupils to respond to one another's work during the writing process helps to bridge the difficult gap between talking and writing. One of the hardest things for the youngest writers to grasp is that the reader is a different person. What s/he knows and understands cannot be taken for granted. Probing and questioning by peer-readers lets the writer know how effectively s/he is communicating ideas.

Peter Hunter (1989) has proposed a hierarchy of concerns which occupy children more or less simultaneously during the writing process. At the highest level is the overall intention, followed by the development of a particular aspect or theme, then detailed elucidation of a specific idea. Lower down the hierarchy comes sentence construction, then concerns about individual words. Lowest of all are spelling and handwriting. Children with learning difficulties frequently become fixated on these lower order skills to the neglect of all others.

We have already seen how the word processor can overcome many spelling and handwriting problems. A built-in thesaurus can help in the search for the right word. Peer-discussion during on-screen drafting can lead to changes in syntax and spark off new ideas. But how can the word processor help to improve higher order skills like the construction of cohesive paragraphs and the sustained development of a theme?

Most word processing programs have a facility for highlighting part of a text, removing it from the screen, and replacing it in a new position. With very little effort, and positively no anguish, children can try out new configurations on the screen. If they don't like what they see they can restore the text to its original state. No more tedious hours spent writing and re-writing. Interestingly, some children – the more superstitious by nature – prefer not to take such risks all at once. For them the physical manipulation of a print-out which has been cut into sections is more acceptable.

To provide practice in the structuring of text teachers may find it useful to create their own files containing material which must be worked on by the pupil:

(1) Beginnings and endings of stories.
(2) Stories for which the dialogue must be written in.
(3) A recipe, or fire-drill, with instructions written in the wrong order.
(4) Headline and subheadings for a newspaper report which must be provided.
(5) A factual account in which only paragraphs-openers + lists of key words appear on screen – children expand the topics.

Paper exercises which require children to insert text inevitably place a limitation on space, whereas a word processing program makes possible any number or length of insertions.

Collaborative writing

The ease with which a computer screen can be viewed by more than one child simultaneously makes joint writing a practicable activity. Of course, this is not to deny that children can collaborate with pencil and paper. However, the physical difficulties of leaning across and looking at someone else's writing and the perceptual problems, particularly for slow readers, of deciphering another's scrawl make it difficult to orchestrate in practice.

There are some modes of writing that particularly lend themselves to joint effort – story-telling, for example, in which children write alternative paragraphs, each one demonstrating some development of the narrative. Rani wrote:

> One day a big tiger escaped from the zoo. His keeper didn't notice and none of the visitors saw him go.

Philip continued:

> He ran down the alley and knocked down the dustbins. Some mothers came out and took the children indoors.

Obviously this works best with third-person narrative and actually encourages a move away from the autobiographical. It can be easier to sustain interest when children are given the opportunity to spark one another off. This is especially useful for children whose own concentration span is limited.

Even more fun is the writing of playscripts when children take on the roles of particular characters and write their own parts. When the first draft is complete it can be printed out, discussed and amendments made. Multiple copies of the final script can be produced, so that the scene can be acted or read in front of the whole class.

One game which utilizes the group power of imagination is 'poetic brainstorming'. The first participant thinks of a subject, preferably one which has some relevance to a current classroom theme or activity. In turn each child is allowed to key in any phrase or single words (maximum 5) which spring to mind. The Enter key is pressed to move the cursor to the next line. When all ideas have been exhausted the 'poem' is read aloud and discussed. At this point the text may be manipulated to produce a pattern or rhythm, and some words may need to be deleted. Even the least able pupil can feel involved in an activity like this and will often find his contributions highly valued.

Classroom management

Aside from the fear many teachers themselves still experience when they come face-to-face with a computer, there is also a belief – usually mistaken – that classroom control will break down with a computer in the room. Most primary schools do not possess a computer per classroom. Machines are usually shared one between two or three classes, perhaps on the basis of a week at a time or on particular days of the week. In the worst cases, a class will have the computer for only one term in the year and afterwards have to behave as if it doesn't exist! The danger is that teachers will begin to view the computer as a foreign object which upsets the usual routine. This need not be so if pupils are initiated into the procedure for 'booting' discs (starting up) and 'logging off' (shutting down).

By and large children accept machines as a normal part of life and there is not much more to turning on the computer than there is to turning on the TV or video recorder. A few basic rules about keeping discs clean, carefully labelled and stored, together with a limitation on the numbers of pupils allowed access to the machine at any one time are all that is needed. It is a good idea to ensure that the keyboard is covered between sessions and that the computer unit is housed in a corner of the classroom well away from sand, water, paint and clay! Having a strict rota-system for pupil use can upset the natural rhythm of composing but may be the only way to make sure that all children have a chance.

Secondary schools are more likely to possess a computer room with a network system (all computers linked to a large-capacity disc-drive and a single printer). I have known teachers stay away from school rather than take their classes to the computer room! Visions of disruptive pupils deliberately pressing all the wrong keys and deleting one another's files are far from reality. Usually the I. T. co-ordinator or a technician is on duty to free the teacher from technical anxieties. Computer screens seem to have a mesmeric effect on most pupils who become entranced at seeing their own words on screen. In my experience lessons in the computer room run themselves. Provided every pupil is organised in advance to have something to compose and a disc on which to save it, the teacher's role is truly one of facilitator rather than instructor.

Teachers writing

Perhaps this point should have been made first. Teachers need to learn to use the word processor themselves if they are to understand fully the benefits of drafting and editing on screen. It is not necessary to act as demonstrator except for children with very poor motor skills. But it is necessary to advise and encourage children to use the screen-writing process to the maxiumum effect. Having participated recently in an intensive three-week course on Writing with Computers, during which we did nothing but write – no technical instructions beyond the bare minimum – I can honestly say that I had never before been truly aware of the degree of thinking that goes into writing. We teachers are required to write all the time, but usually not creatively. We too can become authors, not victims.

Sources of software mentioned

Micro-Electronic Support Unit (MESU), Manchester Polytechnic, Nathersage Road, Manchester, M13 0JA

Concept Keyboard, from AB First, Wharfdale Road, Pentwyn, Cardiff, South Glamorgan, CF2 7HB

Quinkey Microwriter, 31 Southampton Row, London WC1B 5HJ

Pendown, from Logotron Ltd., Dales Brewery, Gwydir Street, Cambridge, CB1 2LJ

Lost Frog from ESM, Duke Street, Wisbech, Cambridgeshire, PE13 2AE

CHAPTER 10

An Approach Through Art

Celia Snaith

> The arts present other forms of reasoning than the purely discursive.
>
> Ken Robinson

The arts, research and dyslexia

Appreciation of the arts in primary education is generally widespread. Creative activities are particularly highly valued in the implementation of cross-curricular and thematic teaching. There is a body of literature on the development of children's art, from which the interested teacher can appreciate significant connections between drawing and writing. However, what appears to me to be lacking, is sufficient work on the specific value of art to help the development of language and literacy for children who find it difficult.

Children normally take to drawing at an early age. Most tend to relinquish it, however, when their critical faculties outstrip their drawing ability. They may then prefer to rely on verbal or formulaic interpretations of what they are trying to record.

Those adults who generally have been educated almost exclusively through the humanities, will probably have given up drawing well before leaving school. There is, after all, no stigma attached to not being able to draw, whereas the opposite is true of being illiterate. Those who are teachers may be unable to give their young pupils a certain kind of help when drawing. It is that form of discussion which encourages them to seek their own solutions to the problems of creating a three-dimensional image on a two-dimensional plane.

112

Alternatively, they may be too tempted to demonstrate certain trick solutions. Furthermore, many of these teachers seem to be a little afraid of art. Perhaps, because of their own excellence in verbal and analytical skills, they may even tend to view children who can draw well, but who are backward at literacy, as of lesser intelligence.

Modern research into the nature of intelligence has led to speculations about the development of the human brain. Discoveries about cerebral dominance and lateralisation of brain functions have stimulated interest in the hemispherical differences in personalities, and the consequent effects on learning patterns in individuals.

Controversial theories abound. From amongst them can be drawn some conclusions which have significant implications for education; and many of these are of considerable interest to anyone concerned about developmental dyslexia.

At the forefront of this neuro-psychological emphasis, two main theories have emerged. The first concerns the *corpus callosum* which is the bundle of fibres linking the two hemispheres. Lesions that might occur during its development can weaken inter-hemispherical connections, creating the need for alternative routes of thought and slower information processing, when, for example, the child is learning to read.

The second of these theories concerns a developmental lag. The language area of the left hemisphere, in what is termed the *angula gyrus*, is supposedly responsible for two specific functions: the fusion of visual and auditory stimuli and the interpretations of abstract symbols. The presence of the male hormone testosterone at a crucial time in the development of the foetus is said to inhibit left-hemisphere growth, thus causing a maturational lag, particularly in boys. Critics, however, who are sceptical of these theories, argue that the incredible plasticity of the developing human brain allows for considerable readjustment of the language area. What is certainly clear is that hemispherical inter-dependence is required, and that some children do have difficulty in cross-modal thinking.

Controversial opinions are also expressed on broader issues. In one perspective (see Pavlidis, pp. 25–26) blame for literacy problems among today's children is partly attributed to the 'total experiences' of film and television. It is suggested that this bombardment of visual and auditory stimuli confuses the less-verbal child, who then prefers to rely on visual thinking, a right-hemisphere prerogative.

In contrast, an American neuro-surgeon involved in split-brain research is critical of the emphasis on verbalisation in education. With the increased necessity for literacy and analytical thought processes, Dr J. R. Bogen (see Springer and Deutsch, p. 17) accuses educators today of neglecting the importance of non-verbal abilities, and the potential contribution of the right brain to a well-balanced mind.

These two conclusions are mirrored, perhaps, by two different aspects of the teaching of reading: the consciously analysed, skill-training approach which formed much of the framework for literacy-teaching in the past; and the broader view in which the pupils are encouraged to make their own discoveries about the way written language works.

Confusing as they might be, all of these perspectives are relevant, in my view, to the teaching of all children, with or without learning difficulties. They are of value to teachers in encouraging them to focus their attention on the *diversity* of children in their classes; of individual differences in preferred modes of thought (visual or verbal) and of their stages of development.

So, whatever the theories of instruction for learning-disabled pupils, whatever persuasions are offered as to the possible neuro-psychological causes of their difficulties, whatever concepts are held about intelligence, and whether or not teachers believe in a brain dysfunction specific to the learning of literacy, the problem in the classroom remains the same. It is how best to cater for individual children who are in difficulties with their own native writing system, (in this case English). How can they be motivated to learn, and then remain confidently in control of their own learning?

I want now to present some ideas for teaching such children, which are based upon the notion that to work through a child's strengths of the right hemisphere will help to develop his or her weaker left-hemisphere functions.

Attitudes to writing

Underachieving children may have some common characteristics of behaviour in the classroom. Problems, such as poor concentration, 'switching off' and hyperactive distractability are among those that are frequently discussed in staff-rooms and between teachers and parents. Many such children will have literacy difficulties, but are often referred to as lazy. They may show promise in areas of general knowledge, and in spatial, non-verbal, creative activities. Some may be clinically clumsy, and a few left-handed; although left-handedness does not necessarily involve attendant learning difficulties.

Confronted with such a child, and having ascertained any relevant information as to the underlying cause of the counter-productive behaviour, the teacher has come to terms with what might be a problematic relationship with the pupil. A pathway towards improving matters has to be found. It is as well to be aware of the possibility of a maturational lag, and of the inter-hemispherical problems mentioned earlier before pronouncing judgement on a lazy child!

Attendant emotional difficulties resulting in severe lack of self-esteem exacerbate the problem. The offer of a task which the child feels can be successfully achieved as well as being enjoyable, not only eliminates the prospect of failure, but it also improves the pupil's relationship with the teacher.

It might seem logical, and indeed, it is often the practice with such children, to coax or demand an attempt at written expression with the promise that, when the work is done, then they may draw a picture. This method, in my view, has several disadvantages. Firstly, it categorises writing as work, but picture-making as play, or at least of lesser importance. Will this attitude not inevitably and adversely affect the child's concept of work?

Secondly, these children are not being helped to recall their experiences and to organise their thoughts in the way which comes most easily to them. That is, through mental imagery. Vygotsky (see N. Martin, p. 166) regarded drawing by the young child as 'first-order symbolism'. Together with imaginative play he saw it as an important factor in the early development of children's written language. L. M. Calkins (1986, pp. 69–70) refers to drawing for young children as a 'predominant form of rehearsal' which leads them into extended paths of the imagination. Writing can then emerge from the oral language which can be triggered off by the initial graphic statement. This is the method traditionally used in the reception class. It surely follows that children who have difficulties in organising language for speech or writing will benefit from an extension period of non-verbal graphic expression before the writing is attempted. I have found this to be so, well into puberty, and even beyond.

Thirdly, from a class-management point of view, the task is made more difficult for the teacher if all children are engaged in writing at the same time. To organise a group of reluctant writers in the pursuit of a creative activity, in preparation for their writing, would give the teacher an opportunity of concentrating on the more confident linguists in the class. Where support or team-teaching is possible, different groups of pupils can be given the adult interaction they need, at the time they need it.

Developmental writing and learning difficulties

The work of Marie Clay (1975) and others who have explored the *development* of learning in language and literacy, has heralded a fresh approach to teaching in our primary schools. It is one in which the child's initial movements of the mark-making tools on the flat surface form the starting point of writing from the earliest stages. With most children this inevitably becomes incorporated into picture-making. The principle has been taken a stage further by Rubens and Newland (1989, p. 17)

> The child's own work is the source of the teaching point used to promote his/her individual development and understanding of language.

Drawing, from direct experience, is shown to have a marked influence on children's perception and interpretation of their environment. It should be understood that this is no new theory, but an implementation of methods advocated many years ago by the promoters of education through art including, notably, Herbert Read, and enriched by the effects of recent research on learning.

Developmental stages in drawing and writing, while they are often parallel, are unlikely to be so on a temporal scale. Yet a correlation between them can be clearly seen to have a beneficial effect one upon the other.

It has already been suggested that certain children may suffer from a maturational lag in the development of the *angular gyrus*. Minimal brain damage to this area of the left hemisphere could be presumed to have a similar effect on the child's ability to learn literacy. The interpretation of *Abstract symbols* seems to be a prime factor here.

Material and stories such as can be found in the *Ginn 360* reading scheme (1984), together with activities such as the invention of codes and pictograms by the children can be of value in helping them to make the transition from pictorial image to sign and abstract symbol. A colleague of mine practises deaf-and-dumb sign language games with his pupils who have normal hearing. This not only broadens their horizons, but probably increases their awareness of the function of symbols.

Open-ended discussion with children about their own picture-making is a good way of helping them to become aware that they have been using symbolism from the moment they discovered the use of the mark-making tool. They can be helped, consciously to understand, for example, that the line they have drawn *stands for* the ground, the circle for the sun, or that the scribble *records* the flight of the aeroplane. Then they may find it easier to recognise letters as standing for sounds, and that writing can represent, not only speech, but thoughts, images and feelings. It is worth observing here that the children we are discussing are often very good, and sometimes superior, at drawing, if their right cerebral functions have developed in compensation for weaknesses in their left hemisphere. This approach, therefore, is encouraging them to learn through their strengths.

Many children with literacy problems may not have experienced this developmental approach on first entering school. If they have been presented with the abstract symbols (letters, sounds, words) in what seems to them to be a meaningless context, they are likely to become confused. They are depressed because they feel that their own problem-solving mechanisms do not work and they are not in control. This may cause them to switch off, and a learning blockage occurs. They will need expert help in reducing their fear and mistrust, by avoidance of all the methods that have failed them so far. Access to *choice* in books, materials and activities will motivate them to work, and to learn. The promotion of success, together with encouragement to find things out by trial and error, prediction and testing, is the main objective.

For children with specific learning difficulties in literacy who *have* been introduced to reading and writing through a developmental approach, a more structured, skill-training method might be appropriate, alongside an enabling and child-centred learning situation. Beverly Mathias, of the National Library for the Handicapped Child, has this to say about reading books:

> We believe that real books, as opposed to reading scheme books will help a child to read more easily, though sometimes children who have a disability with language need that extra push with something structured at the beginning.
>
> (Goodenough, 1989, pp. 118–119)

Looking, drawing, writing, reading

> Looking leads to scientific, spiritual and historical experiences ...
> Looking through drawing prolongs the looking.
>
> (Rubens and Newland, 1989, p. 17)

There is a wide range of child-centred creative and problem-solving activities, all of which can be used as initial stimuli for the flow of language and the development of literacy. I might refer to pattern-making, model-building, the use of colour, drama, music or dance in the wider context of integrated studies in the primary classroom. However, I am restricting this discussion to the use of drawing in language development for reasons which include, most importantly, those statements about *looking* quoted above.

● Learning how to look is learning how to learn.
● Drawing is closely connected to writing.
● It engages the mind and aids concentration.
● It is an easily organised activity, especially in the primary classroom.
● Last, but not least, it is simple to reproduce for publication.

Two main types of drawing will be considered:

(1) Drawing from the *imagination* which employs mental imagery and visual memory.
(2) Observational drawing, from direct experience which involves either close and careful scrutiny, or instant noting down of significant features.

Both types of drawing activity are valuable as initial stimuli for talking and writing.

It is my opinion that, for many children, the skills of reading can be acquired most accessibly through their own drawing and writing. It goes without saying that beautiful books, of all kinds, must fill the learning environment for young children; and that poring over books being read to, shared and paired reading should be high in the curriculum. But to dictate or to write their own stories and non-fiction statements from the very beginning, to illustrate and 'publish' them as books in the classroom, will give children a real purpose for writing and something vital to read when they are done.

The Organisation of form

All graphic statements made by children stem from an innate desire to organise form and to create some kind of tangible symbols-system through which their personal understanding of phenomena might be read. To make sense of the environment and of the inner feelings with which the individual responds to that sensory array, is basic to human nature. Drawing especially helps children to reflect upon their perceptions, and when the artifact is seen to have an impact upon other individuals, the statement becomes external communication. Some examples of work by junior school children with special educational needs might serve to illustrate my points. The first piece of writing emerged from the child's initial desire to create order out of a jumble of plastic letters, and from the dialogue which followed.

Louise was a left-handed eight-year-old with learning difficulties and severe lack of self-esteem. At an individual session in which an attempt was being made to tackle her problems with literacy, she was presented with a set of plastic letters, and asked if she could make any words. Her first and immediate attack on the letters was to arrange them into colour groups. This was probably an activity with which she had become familiar in the infant classes, giving her, therefore, a sense of security and confidence in her own ability. Her spontaneous action was also an indication of her positive delight in manipulating colour.

Presently some words emerged, carefully set out in a preferred colour sequence; *lykl, cat, bed, pour*. The first was a deliberate attempt at *little*, but she could not say what she had meant with *pour*, and asked to be told the word. Confusing it with the word *paw*, she created, with some judicious help, the little 'story' which appears in figure 10.1. All the words were built with the plastic letters, and considerable ingenuity was exercised when she ran out of a *w* and a *t*. She substituted *m* and *f* respectively, knowing full well that they were the wrong letters turned upside down and reversed to make do, so that she could finish her work. Louise then copied the corrected sentence, and illustrated it. In her case, the drawing came afterwards, the mental picture having arisen from her arrangement of the coloured letters; but the important point is that the writing was stimulated by her own creative approach to the organisation of form, and that a real sense of achievement was the result. This piece of work could well have initiated the start of a book-making project in the classroom.

When the piece of work, either under way or completed, is presented to the class, or to a group of peers, the teacher or adult helper can draw the children out in verbal description and expansion of ideas. This sharing of talking and listening is valuable in linguistic development. A tape-recorder in operation during this session can be helpful to the teacher, for reference, when he or she is planning the next consultation with the child. Further attempts at writing may be made by the child, with an adult acting as scribe, or, with the collaboration of a more confident pupil-writer. The preparation of the book can lead to a

17·9·87·

a little cat sat
on a bed
to eat cake
with her xxoo
paws xxxooo

Figure 10.1 Writing originally constructed in plastic letters, and illustration by Louise

whole range of craft, design and technological processes for the enrichment of the learning environment and for the ultimate satisfaction and increased self-esteem of the child in question.

Observational drawings and language

The drawings and writing shown in figures 2 and 3 were executed by two younger junior children from Annandale Primary School. The

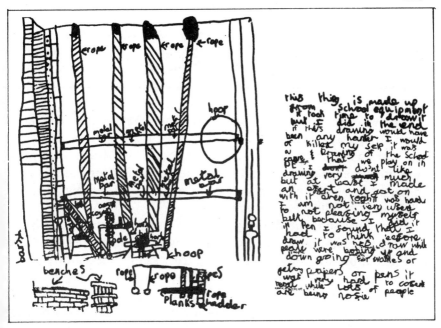

Figure 10.2

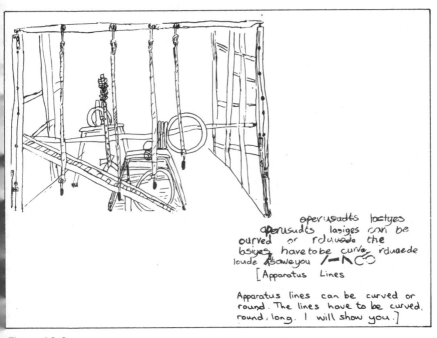

Figure 10.3

had been taking part in an experimental project in which the whole school were asked to draw the complicated arrangement of P.E. apparatus and then to write about the experience. The results were published in a booklet by the I.L.E.A. Art and Design Centre (*Developmental Writing, Developmental Drawing* I.L.E.A. 1986). A comparison of these two pieces of work is interesting.

The writing in figure 2 is fluent and most expressive of the child's emotional reaction to the difficult task. The cursive handwriting is well set out, and includes two self-corrections. The drawing is more primitive than the other child's, and he or she felt the need to label different items of the paraphernalia. Here, it seems, is a highly verbal child who is diffident about drawing.

In comparison, the drawing in figure 3 is more mature. It is the writing that I find so interesting. Writing is obviously more difficult for this child, but the content tells us the truly significant features of the visual array. The final remark 'I will show you /‑∧ℂ0' reinforces this, and indicates that there is no need to say more. The drawing tells all. It is possible that the pupil did not know what to say, and that a teacher helped the child to express ideas in language by means of consultation. Nevertheless, I think that the salient point here is that this is a truly spatially-orientated child, perhaps less verbal, but whose strengths at drawing can well be harnessed in extending his or her verbal language development.

Lee is in the top junior class in a special school for children with moderate learning difficulties. There is a history of illiteracy in his family background. He is timid and despondent when it comes to reading and writing but he has a lively mind and his oral language is good. At this school great importance is attached to the value of educational visits, and these occur at least once a week. Lee's own remark in appreciation of school visits was that 'it gives us experience' The illustration in figure 10.4 is of a page from his diary of events in relation to a theme on transport. The observational drawings were made on site at Gatwick airport. The writing is a fair copy worked on the jumbo typewriter. It may seem anecdotal and colourless, but it must be remembered that his literacy problems are severe. The drawings are full of information, and the writing a considerable achievement. Further discussion with Lee about his drawings could well induce some extended language.

Paul, in the same class as Lee, dictated to his teacher 'I *panicked* when I saw the 737, as if I were on it myself'. This emotive word could become the source of a whole variety of teaching points, from context

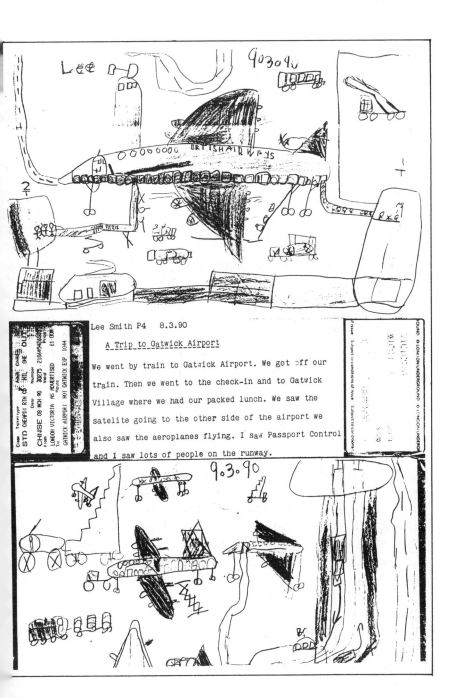

Lee Smith P4   8.3.90

A Trip to Gatwick Airport

We went by train to Gatwick Airport. We got off our
train. Then we went to the check-in and to Gatwick
Village where we had our packed lunch. We saw the
satelite going to the other side of the airport we
also saw the aeroplanes flying. I saw Passport Control
and I saw lots of people on the runway.

Figure 10.4

and meaning to spelling patterns and syllabication, depending on individual need and stage of development. For example:

```
P  A  N  I  C  K  E  D        P  A  N  I  C
M  A  N                          M  A  G  I  C
R  A  N                          M  U  S  I  C
   A  N  D                    P  I  C  N  I  C
H  A  N  D                       T  O  P  I  C
S  T  A  N  D
         P  I  C  K  E  D
      T  R  I  C  K  E  D              ETC.
```

Paul actually drew the control tower 'because it was easier', but his graphic record of the experience brought back the memory of his emotional reaction, enabling him to express his feelings in such pertinent terms.

It is most important that children should have opportunities of expressing their inner feelings through the arts, oral and written language. In the effort to cover syllabuses and national curriculum attainment targets, sufficient space for this is easily overlooked. But emotion represents the mainspring of learning, and children encouraged to declare their feelings in art and in writing will develop their literacy.

> The creative arts engage, educate and at the same time free the whole person to have fuller and more disciplined use of all his powers . . .
> (Harriet Proudfoot, Blenkin and Kelly, p. 119)

Ben, aged seven, was the youngest of three intelligent children. He was a quiet and thoughtful boy, aware of his own good general knowledge and oral language development. He was, however, at the time of producing the piece of writing below, extremely worried about his difficulties. His problems were exacerbated by parental anxiety and as his specific learning disabilities in literacy were very apparent, this anxiety was understandable. The recent traumatic experience of a serious fire at his home must have increased his emotional vulnerability. He had made a painting of a church with a cross. Then he wrote:

The Cross

The cross is to rmember Jesues.
And the pepole how bleave in Jesus
And I ust to go to church.
And it was in the BB hall

And you get a juper and a book to mark.
On Fridy and I ust to hav a book and till
the housr bert Down but my juper was saft in the fure and tody me
and my bruther hav to go again to BB. (*Boys Brigade*)

It seems to me that the emotional release provided by the painting enabled Ben to clarify his thoughts and to express them in these subtle and philosophical terms. The writing was unaided and the most extensive piece he had achieved hitherto.

We have looked at some samples of children's work as the immediate result of direct experience. Ben's painting was produced through the vivid memory of an emotional happening (his precious jumper was *saved* from the fire!). The following examples are concerned with drawings which indicate the use of mental imagery with three different objectives:

● the recording of information through drawings where writing is particularly difficult;
● the development of memory for grapho-phonic correspondences;
● the fostering of the development of ideas while composing a piece of imaginative writing.

Edward, at thirteen, now attends a special boarding school. He has severe reading and writing problems, but he is able to answer questions and to record observations, unaided, via drawings and minimally written notes. Figure 10.5 gives an example of work done for his prep on feeding birds and the dispersal of seeds.

James was twelve and had specific learning difficulties in literacy. The designing of his own pictograms helped him considerably in the recall of vowel digraphs and their grapho-phonic indications. Figure 10.6 is a reproduction of this boy's original designs. There is wit and talent demonstrated in the way he has incorporated the letters into the graphic symbol. This is the kind of activity which can help those children who have problems in the interpretation of abstract symbols, as indeed was the case with James.

Figure 10.7 shows an example of drawing worked in the middle of a rough draft for a piece of creative writing, also by James at twelve years. He had come to a point where he was at a loss as to how to proceed. It was suggested to him that he should spend some time sketching the situation as he saw it in his mind's eye. He was then able to develop further ideas in writing.

126

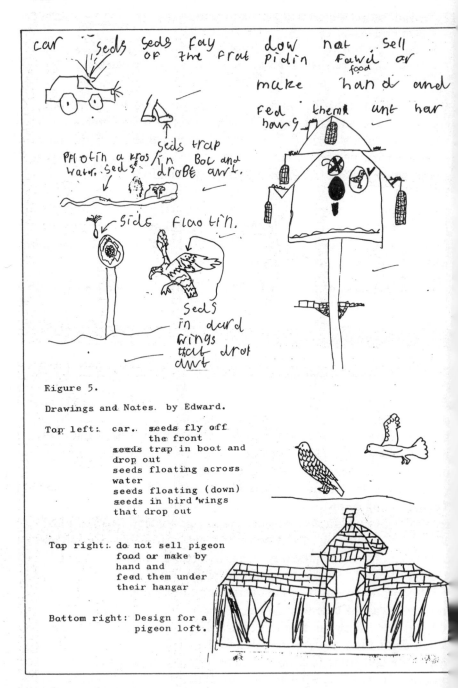

Figure 5.

Drawings and Notes. by Edward.

Top left: car. seeds fly off
           the front
           seeds trap in boot and
           drop out
           seeds floating across
           water
           seeds floating (down)
           seeds in bird 'wings
           that drop out

Top right: do not sell pigeon
           food or make by
           hand and
           feed them under
           their hangar

Bottom right: Design for a
              pigeon loft.

Figure 10.5

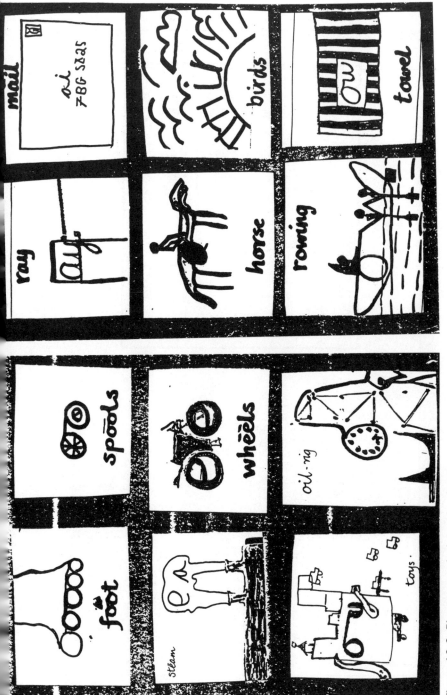

Figure 10.6 Pictograms designed by James

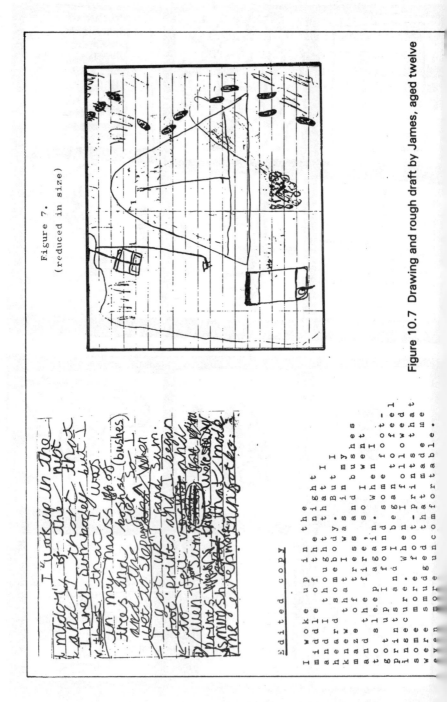

Figure 7.
(reduced in size)

Edited copy

I woke up in the
middle of the night
and I thought that I
heard somebody. But I
knew that I was in my
maze of tress and bushes
and the
to sleep again. When I
got up I found some foot-
prints and I began to feel
insecure. When I followed
some more foot-prints that
were smudged that made me
even more uncomfortable.

Figure 10.7 Drawing and rough draft by James, aged twelve

James is, in fact, becoming a competent creative writer with the aid of a word processor. The extract in Figure 10.8 from an extensive story composed when he was thirteen, gives a flavour of his growing use of written language. Since it seems to reflect and develop that germ of an idea contained in the sketch and scribble from one year previously, I feel that it might encourage teachers of pupils such as James. For his

It was starting to get dark when we got to the edge of the woods. The vast trunks of the redwoods made dark shadows in the moonlight. There was no sound except for our footsteps, as we walked together back to our camp. As we moved through the patches of darkness and light we sang a song but we soon stopped because the silence was too great.

I heard a sound behind us like giant footsteps – thud, thud, thud. We stopped and the sound stopped too. We started to walk faster and the thudding footsteps speeded up. We were all scared and our hearts began to thump.

It got darker as we got further into the forest and to our relief the thudding stopped. We decided it had been our imaginations so we started singing again – a cheery song to keep our spirits up. As we followed the track round the corner there was a crashing through the undergrowth as a vast shadow loomed up to the side of our leader.

Figure 10.8 Extract of creative writing by James at thirteen years

was the case of a child who had completely failed to meet the expected pattern of development in literacy throughout his primary school years. He was the typical shoulder-shrugging individual whose utter embarrassment and lack of self-esteem had made life difficult, for himself and his teachers. Just to have abandoned all the methods which appeared to have failed him, to view him in a different light, and to give him real credit for the very good things he could do, seem to have spurred him on to renewed efforts. Was this the turning point towards an alternative route to learning in a dyslexic child, or simply a case of maturational lag?

130

Conclusion

> Special needs is a metaphor for what children should be doing as a whole.
>
> (Peter Brinson, Goodenough, p. 122)

What is needed for communication is a flow of ideas. Art, being very much a form of internal communication, prompts opportunities for the teacher once the flow is generated. Tapping in to the child's internal communication can make it external. It is like getting into the child's mind to convince him or her that:

- success is attainable;
- the process will be enjoyable;
- no security will be lost in feeling, as yet, self-sufficient in his or her thinking processes.

On the contrary, the latter will be enriched and expanded. A deal is being made with the child to come out of a closed situation. In addition, there often appears to be a gap in the connections between the two hemispheres, and it is the left, verbalising one that is underfunctioning. Activities, therefore, that utilize the right brain, and which can lead to, or incorporate spoken language will help the two hemispheres to work together.

Generally speaking then, this approach springs from a prompting of expressions from the child's experiences; distilling them into some recognizable form, graphic, verbal or both, and working through these towards a written realization. Therefore, for children with learning difficulties just as for all others, their own direct or imaginative experiences become the material on which language and literacy can be founded.

NOTE: The drawings illustrated in Figures 2 and 3 are reproduced by kind permission of Maurice Rubens and Mary Newland, M.B.E.

CHAPTER 11

The Use of Names in Early Literacy

Anne Washtell

> Print is not straightforward. There is much that young children need to understand, yet most of this understanding is bound up in their previous experience and in what they themselves bring to the task.
>
> (*English for Ages 5-11*, 1988, p. 7)

Names and early learning

In the Autumn of 1987 I taught a class of reception and middle infant children (rising five to six year olds). During the first weeks with the class, I decided to observe and record a range of insights that the children were displaying about literacy. It quickly became apparent that through their use of *Names*, many children were able to explore some of their ideas about reading and writing in concrete, meaningful contexts.

I noticed for example, that the children enjoyed making lists of names and would do this time and time again. The activity appeared to be carried out as a means to an end, with the children also gaining a great deal of satisfaction from reading their lists out to each other. More often than not, however, they would spontaneously draw on names in order to point out commonalities in words. This would often occur most unexpectedly: during lesson times; whilst they were lining up; as we moved around the school and also in the street. For example, Samuel studied a greetings card which said 'Goodbye and Good Luck'. He pointed to the 'L' in 'Luck' and proudly announced 'Miss. Look! That says Lee.' (Lee was the name of another boy in the class.)

What cannot be stressed enough is his sheer delight in making this discovery.

On another occasion whilst browsing informally through Brian Wildsmith's book *The Cat on the Mat*, Jos*eph* commented 'Hey Miss! My name's in el*eph*ant!' Another time, Corah had to wait a few moments before I was free to talk to her. So, she sat patiently in the Book Corner, casually picked up a pile of exercise books and faultlessly read out all the names on the covers 'Kartik, Sinead, Reuben...' When I asked her how she could do this, she immediately responded, 'I know where everyone puts their books in the trays.' Corah had only been in school a few weeks and, from my initial assessments, was only in the beginning stages of reading. But here she was demonstrating her capabilities as a reader, drawing on the context of the 'tidy drawers' to help her. Even more remarkable was the fact that half the tidy drawers were not visible from where she was sitting!

Obviously, something of great importance is going on for these young children, demonstrated through the way they operate on names. A major concern appears to be to impose personal meaning over print by seeking out familiar letters and recognising patterns, with names providing the anchor for their hypotheses. Names evidently play a small but significant part in children's early literacy experiences. Teachers who are ready to pay attention to this fact will be able to build upon the expertise that children reveal when using them.

Through the careful observation of these often self-initiated 'literacy events', (for example by using The Diary of Observations from the ILEA's *Primary Language Record*, 1988), it is possible to say with a degree of certainty that a child is clearly making progress, and showing development, however small the steps might be. This was crystalised for me by looking at many of the children's informal experiences over time, but it was one child in particular, Katrina, who taught me to recognise and value her efforts as she began to gain control over her own literacy. Through making regular observations I gradually learned how to view literacy from her point of view, and so was enabled to redefine my role as her teacher in order to promote and support her efforts to become independent.

The work of Heath (1983), Payton (1984) and others has pointed to the importance of community and local environment as well as the home in the shaping of the child's literacy. Significantly, Heath's findings suggest that the pre-school experiences of literacy of two of the communities in her study were apparently inappropriate for preparing children for the literacy of school.

I think an awareness of Heath's argument is helpful when considering what is on offer and what is considered appropriate within the classroom 'literacy club'. Being aware of the dangers of my own preconceptions and maintaining a much more open minded attitude certainly helped me to recognise that a knowledge of names, amongst many other equally valid experiences, was part of the luggage that children brought with them to school and which they unquestioningly assumed would come in useful. My entries in the *Primary Language Record* (PLR) highlighted the importance of names for many children in the class and set me thinking as to why this should be.

The significance of names in early literacy has been acknowledged in research over the years although more often than not, it has not been given a central focus. Names are important to children and highly charged with personal meaning. If children meet names in natural everyday situations and contexts, their insights into their own literacy will arise in ways that make sense to them. Traditionally, teaching children to write their name has been a universal focus in the first weeks of any new reception class. After all, to be able to write one's own name has historically been viewed as the 'mark of literacy'. Writing over fifty years ago Gertrude Hildreth (1936) suggested that the extent to which a child could write his/her name was an 'indication of mental maturity'. Teachers and parents alike have always known that being able to write his/her name is a milestone in a child's cognitive development.

Marie Clay (1975) offers some valuable insights into children's name writing. She sees signatures, for example, as 'very personal signs' and claims, not surprisingly, that for most children their name is the first conventional writing that a child learns. Here Clay's views coincide with those of Ferreiro and Teberovsky (1983). At first, Clay argues, the child recognises the initial letter (a capital) of his name as a sign' Clay, 1975, p. 44). Here her notion of the 'sign concept' helps to clarify the significance of name writing, for when children have understood the 'sign concept' they have come to the vital realisation that print stands for something besides itself. It is when the child writes his/her name fully, Clay argues, that a '. . . transition from letters as signs to words as signs' is made (Clay, 1975, p. 47). It is in this complex area of understanding the arbitrary nature of signs that many children struggle, continuing to do so in some cases, for a very long time. It is in this aspect of literacy that, I believe, names can play a very special role.

Name is central to the child's growing knowledge and understanding of identity and place in the social and symbolic order of the world. From the onset of life, the child can be seen to be involved in the process of constructing identity and discovering who he/she is, in relation to the 'significant others' in their life. Naming is central to this process of understanding and clarification. From birth onwards, names play a significant and natural part in the child's early exploration of language and literacy within the home and local environment.

Names are highly meaningful to all of us throughout our lives. This is especially true for children who are still in the process of 'naming the world' when they come to school. Perhaps adults pay too little attention to this sensitivity.

When a child starts school it is through the constant and frequent contact with names, and the special ways in which they are used in school, that she/he is initiated into this new society. This induction process is vital to help children to reconstruct their identity into that of pupil. It could be argued that name eases the transition from child to pupil by providing security and stability during this process. Although some of the experiences of naming will resemble those that took place in early childhood, others that a child meets in school, for example, the Register, will be new and different.

If we stop and think about it, names are everywhere in school. The classroom and cloakroom are littered with name labels on coatpegs, exercise books, plant pots, work on the walls, tidy drawers and so on. They are also of course to be found in the Book Corner – inside books as well as on front covers.

What I want to show through Katrina is that names are very real to the child's own world and also form a natural part of classroom life. Secondly, that this sense of relevance gives great contextual force to children's initial encounters with names in print. Most importantly names help children to understand that print carries meaning – enables them to see the relationship between a written symbol and an actual person. This, as I will show with Katrina, is the significance of names.

Katrina: a child who used names

In discussing Katrina's experiences, it is important to stress that her encounters centring on Name, sit within a complex web of many other everyday literary experiences typical of any reception class child and that the instances examined here are a small but significant part of her growing awareness of herself as a reader and a writer.

Katrina joined my class just before her fifth birthday, remaining with me for four full terms. At first she appeared to lack confidence and my preliminary observations of her suggested that she apparently had very little knowledge of reading and writing. However, from the beginning, she indicated through her preferred activities that learning to read and write were a high priority for her.

Looking back at my observational records and the samples of her writing, the main emphasis of this account will focus on her development as a writer, although inevitably we also gain glimpses of her growing confidence as a reader. The range of her writing can be categorised as follows:

- Learning to write her name, which dominated her first five months in school.
- Persistently practising her handwriting which continued throughout the four terms.
- Making numerous cards to take home to her family or to give to friends.
- Writing her own stories (she did not want stories written down for her by an adult).
- Writing poetry and rhymes (this started towards the end of her time at the school).
- Making lists of all the words that she knew.
- Making lists of names, which eventually developed into the making of Registers.
- Bringing to school a steady stream of 'home writing'.

This list provides an overall feel of the breadth of her writing whilst indicating Katrina's priorities in her learning and most importantly her interests, i.e. home and school. It might be helpful to know that much of Katrina's writing was self-initiated, some of it undertaken during 'choice' times. Not surprisingly, a common thread running through her self-initiated writing was her use of names.

In this account I have decided to concentrate particularly on Katrina's efforts to learn to write her name and on her decision to keep Registers. Learning to write her name was chosen for a number of reasons. First of all, because it proved to be a struggle for Katrina; secondly, because it taught me so much about the teacher's role and thirdly, because it is generally acknowledged to provide children with their first conventionally spelt word and therefore has a key part to play in children's literacy development. Katrina's first Register has been chosen for close analysis because it too reveals the concerns and interests of a child just starting school. First of all though, it will be interesting to consider Katrina's attitude towards learning as this has a bearing on the two literacy events.

It soon became apparent that Katrina wanted to take an active part in her own learning and that she was unwilling, sometimes to the point of anger, to sit back and let others do things for her. However, she was also a keen observer, especially if another child was reading to me. She would appear within seconds of a child starting to share a book with me and settle herself to watch closely and try to help. At story time, she would position herself near the front of the group and always listened attentively. She also enjoyed sharing reading with 'Big Books' and would take a keen interest in 'Shared Writing' sessions, although her contributions were not frequent. Most of all, she simply loved me to read to her, particularly her favourite books, *Each Peach Pear Plum*, *Rosie's Walk* and *Peace at Last*.

Learning to write her name was an urgent preoccupation for Katrina and proved to be a laborious experience. In this aspect of writing, she sought my help frequently. Her earliest attempts, (see Example 11.1 and 11.2) show that she experienced great difficulty with the formation of 'K' and also in trying to copy the rest of her name.

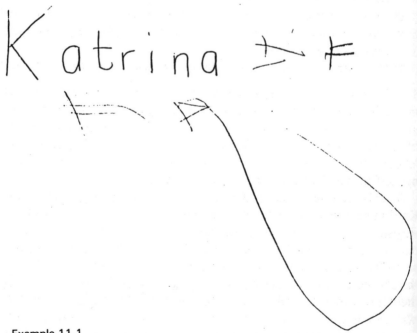

Example 11.1

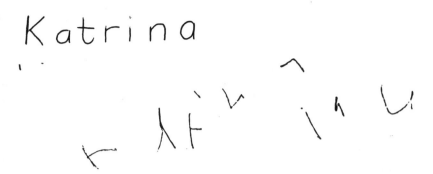

Example 11.2

However, I noted in my Diary of Observations that in the third week, Katrina told me how to help her:

> Katrina very anxious to learn to write her name. 'Write my name Miss.' Katrina frustrated by difficulty in writing her name. 'I can't do it.' We tried together (at her request) me holding my hand lightly over hers as we formed the letters.

By November 1987, Katrina succeeded in copying her own name, still with a great deal of difficulty and from this experience, we had an illuminating discussion also noted in my Diary: 'talked and named letters which she found "easy" e.g. "i" and "a".' These letters began to occur frequently in her independent writing (see Example 11.3). Katrina would generate strings of letters which she called writing and was very satisfied with the result.

Example 11.3

By the following January, Katrina would confidently call out the letters of her name for me to write and at the beginning of February 1988, she was writing her full name independently. From this point on, she truly blossomed as a writer. For Katrina, being able to write her name was a highly liberating experience (see Example 11.4). She had gained her independence, which meant that she could write and write and write – which is just what she did!

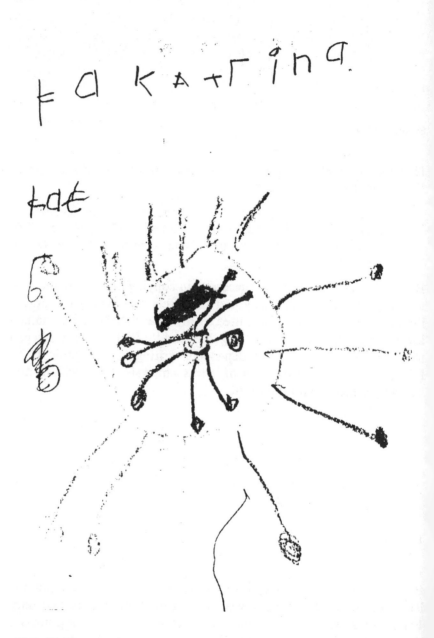

Example 11.4

It can be seen from this account, that Katrina had indicated the need for several different approaches to help her learn how to write her name. She would ask me to write her name and then she would try to copy it; she would dictate the letters to me so that she could watch how I wrote it and she would ask me to hold her hand to help her feel how to write it. She worked independently as well, practising certain letters over and over again until she was satisfied. What is so interesting is that these initiatives from Katrina came in spite of the daily practice that I had planned for her. She was teaching me that what she needed from me was versatility, flexibility and most important of all – variety. For me as a teacher to try to rely on a single approach to this task was

Example 11.5

certainly not going to provide enough information for Katrina, if she was ultimately to succeed.

It is also interesting to note that Katrina could spell out the letters of her name as well as identify it on charts and notices in the classroom long before she could write it all down. On one occasion she complained bitterly that another teacher had written her name wrongly on a chart. Close scrutiny and a heated discussion between herself and her classmate Corah, quickly identified the problem. The teacher's error was to have written the 'r' and 'i' too closely together so that they looked like an 'n'. This simply would not do for Katrina who was by now an expert on the letter formation in her name! These kind of incidents emphasise the need for teachers to be looking at the processes in learning, not just the products. Katrina was demonstrating that she knew much more about her name than she yet could produce on paper and said so with authority and conviction.

Running concurrently with learning to write her name, Katrina began to write independently, frequently drawing on letters in her name.

This early sample dated September 1987, shows evidence of 'K' (see Example 11.5) but no message. By March 1988, she is making patterns with the letters of her name, particularly 'a', 'i' and 'n' – the letters she had told me that she found easy to write. Around this time she experimented with altering the first letters of her name 'Gotrina', 'Matrina', 'Natrina', etc. (see Example 11.6).

As Ferreiro and Teberosky (1983) explain, the child's name does seem to have 'a very special function' at the beginning because it does provide a 'prototype' for future pieces of written language. Most importantly, they suggest that it provides children with their 'first stable string' of letters which is crucial to future development. Their findings certainly seem to be borne out by Katrina's early development in school.

The collecting of names and making of registers

From the outset Katrina became an avid collector of names and an active list maker, although she would also generate strings of letters in her story writing or practice writing. She seemed to take a keen interest in names as entities in themselves. Lists of names were made at home as well as at school and would proudly be shown to me. Later on, her listing of names for no apparent reason switched into the desire to keep Registers. She made at least seven registers which she used during the

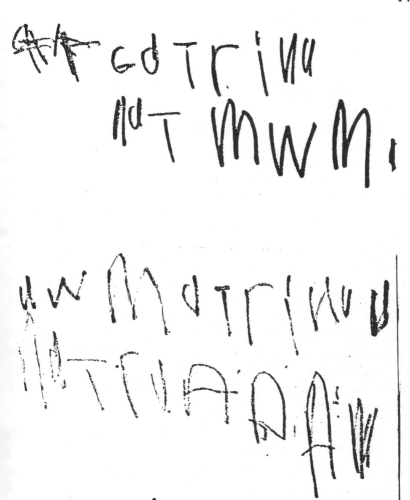

xample 11.6

me I knew her. I will now discuss her first register in some detail,
tting out first of all the circumstances in which it arose.
  Katrina told me that she wanted to make a register and that she
tended to go round the class and ask them to write their names down
or her. She explained that she wanted to work independently, firmly
jecting any offers of assistance from me and rapidly organised
erself with a blank book from the 'Writing Corner'. The rest of the
ass, who were to play a significant role in this literary event, were
gaged in a variety of activities.

This literacy event falls into three parts:

- Katrina's decision to make a register;
- the manner in which she collected the Names;
- the brief discussion which she spontaneously held with me towards the end of the activity.

Her decision to make a register was a surprise departure from her usual routine of simply collecting lists of names. This was a promising initiative as it offered the potential of being a purposeful piece of writing. For quite some time, Katrina could be observed as she slowly made her way around the class, patiently explaining to children what she was trying to do, and asking them to write their names into her register. The event seemed to be a highly sociable activity and Katrina was obviously enjoying herself carrying out the task. Her message was unchanging as she approached each child: 'I'm making a register. Write me your name.' She would then stand quietly, watching closely as the other children wrote their names down for her. (The register although faint, is reproduced below. See Example 11.7).

I was also included in this process and was asked to write down the names of two other teachers as well. We discussed whether she wanted first or second names, and Katrina settled on first. It was after I had written 'Anne' and 'Penny' that she made a fascinating comparison about our names:

> You and Miss Tuxford have got 'n's and one of these ('e') (quoted from my Diary of Observations).

I told Katrina that the name of the letter was 'e' which she promptly went on to spot in other names on her list.

It is interesting to note the dual purpose of this activity: on the one hand, her expressed aim was to make a register and on the other she was carefully studying the letter patterns, noting similarities and differences. Talking about our names gave Katrina the opening that she needed to demonstrate how skilled she was in analysing words. Her still limited knowledge of the letter names of the alphabet was appropriately utilised and she was not in the least daunted by the fact that she did not know the name of the letter 'e'. This brief exchange with me, lasted at most thirty seconds but provided an excellent opportunity for her to test out her knowledge and for me to monitor her progress.

The social aspect of this activity deserves some comment, for it would seem that through the making of her register Katrina was

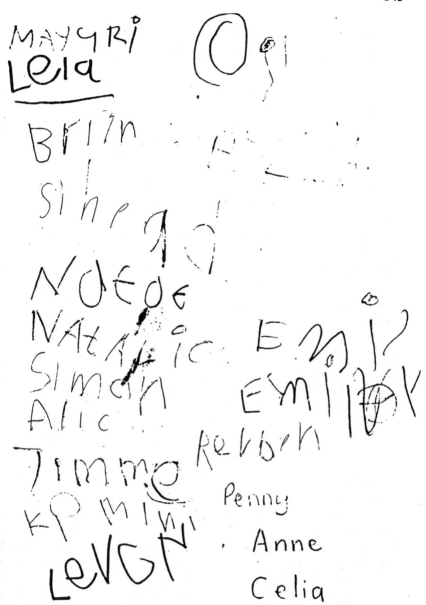

Mayuri, Lela, Bryn, Sinead, Kartik, Natalie, (who started to write her name twice), Simon, Alice, Timmie, Kamini, Devon, Emily (who started to write her name twice), Penny, Anne, and Celia (the last three names of teachers written down at Katrina's request by me).

Example 11.7

helping herself to organise her understanding of this new world of school. It is worth thinking for a few moments just why registers are so fascinating to children. First of all, twice a day, with routine regularity, registers publicly acknowledge the child's identity and sense of belonging within the class. For teachers, taking the register is so routine that we hardly give it a second thought. Yet children listen and respond to the register, day in and day out, perhaps not really understanding its purpose. However, as with a favourite story children are quick to pick up errors or notice any deviations, for example, if someone is away.

Because they follow a predictable pattern, registers are a familiar reliable, largely unchanging source of information about the processes of reading and writing and this is one of the reasons that I believe Katrina was attracted to them. I think that through registers, Katrina was able actively to pursue the relationship between hearing a name called out, seeing it read and watching a written mark placed beside it. Time and time again she was in a position to observe me demonstrate through marking the register, that print holds meaning, but more importantly, to help consolidate this understanding; the people whose names are represented in written language, are physically present also (i.e. her friends).

In the making of this first register it would seem that Katrina was concerned with two things; firstly, her growing understanding of her identity within the class, and secondly, her developing realisation that print stands for something in its own right. In other words Katrina was discovering that print holds meaning. I believe that in the keeping of her lists and registers, Katrina was able to hypothesise about this issue over time, and to practise, within self-imposed limits which made sense to her, in order to make this understanding her own.

Finally, I believe that Katrina's friends played a very special role in the creation of her first register. When Katrina compiled the register she behaved rather like an autograph hunter, asking her friends to write their names. In previous name lists she had copied names from 'tidy drawer' labels, but on this occasion that approach did not serve her purposes. Seeing the different names written in different hands meant that each child was leaving their own very individual mark in her book. This enabled Katrina quickly to identify one name from another and she found to her delight that she could reread her list with speed and with great confidence.

Conclusion

It has only been possible to trace one or two of Katrina's experiences with Name in this study. However, it can be said with certainty that after a slow and unconfident start, Katrina soon began to make clear progress in her reading and writing. The key lessons that she taught me were the importance of setting her own pace, the need for self-initiated activities (including practice); opportunities for her to take an observational role and most importantly the support and collaboration of her classmates and teacher. An underlying theme of this account has been the value for teachers in observing the small literacy events as well as the more obvious activities. For it is in these scraps of evidence that we can provide proof of progress in those children whose development is slow.

As I said at the beginning of this piece, Name forms a tiny fragment in the mosaic of children's literacy, but in my opinion is no less significant for that. I would not wish to claim that Name alone helped Katrina in her early literacy experiences although I think that it certainly played its part. For all children, the ultimate goal in literacy must be independence; perhaps names go some way towards enabling children to achieve the necessary control and ultimately, empowerment.

Children's books referred to in the chapter

Ahlberg, J. and S. A. (1980). *Each Peach Pear Plum*. Picture Lions.
Hutchins, P. (1970). *Rosie's Walk*. Bodley Head.
Murphy, J. (1980). *Peace at Last*. Picturemac.
Wildsmith, B. (1982) *The Cat on the Mat*. Oxford.

References

Abbs, P. (ed.) (1987). *Living Powers: The Arts in Education.* Lewes: Falmer.
Albes, Z. M. (1981). *The Child Under Stress: Dyslexia.* London: Granary.
Alland, A. (1983). *Playing with Form.* Columbia, USA: Columbia University Press.
Alston, J. and Taylor, J. (1987). *Handwriting: Theory, Research and Practice.* London: Croom Helm.
Arnold, H. (1982). *Listening to Children Reading.* London: Hodder & Stoughton.
Augur, J. (1989). 'Parental Involvement with Spelling'. In Pinsent, P. (ed.) *Spotlight on Spelling.* Bicester: A. B. Academic Publishers.
Ayres, A. J. (1972). *Sensory Integration and Learning Disorders.* California: Western Psychological Services.
Barrs, M. *et al.* (1990). *Patterns of Learning: The Primary Language Record and the National Curriculum.* London: CLPE.
Barrs, M. *et al.* (1989). *The Primary Language Record: Handbook for Teachers.* London: ILEA.
Beard, R. (1984). *Children's Writing in the Primary School.* London: Hodder & Stoughton.
Beard, R. (1987). *Developing Reading 3-13.* London: Hodder & Stoughton.
Bedford, S. (1987). *Helping Clumsy Children with Handwriting: A Multi-Disciplinary Viewpoint.* Stratford-upon-Avon: NCSE.
Blakeslec, T. R. (1980). *The Right Brain.* London: Macmillan.
Blenkin, G. M. and Kelly, A. V. (1983). *The Primary Curriculum in Action.* London: Harper & Row.
Bloom, W. (1987). *Partnership with Parents in Reading.* London: Hodder & Stoughton.
Boden, T. (ed.) (1982). *Learning Through Art in the Primary School.* Leicester: Leicestershire Educational Committee.
Boettcher, J. (1978). *An Ideal Remedial Reading Program.* Paper presented at the Annual Meeting of the International Reading Association (Houston, Texas, May 1-5, 1978).

Bradley, L. (1980). *Assessing Reading Difficulties. A Diagnostic and Remedial Approach.* London: Macmillan.

Bradley, L. (1981). 'The Organisation of Motor Patterns for Spelling: An Effective Remedial Strategy for Backward Readers'. *Developmental Medicine and Child Neurology*, **23**: 83–91.

Bradley, L. and Bryant, P. (1983). 'Categorising Sound and Learning to Read – a Causal Connection'. *Nature*, **301**: 419–421.

Brand, V. (1988). *Spelling Made Easy: Multi-sensory Structured Spelling.* Baldock, Herts: Egon Publishers.

Brown, G. (1982). 'The Spoken Language'. In Carter, R. (ed.) *Linguistics and the Teacher.* London: Routledge.

Bryant, P. and Bradley, L. (1985). *Children's Reading Problems: Psychology and Education.* Oxford: Blackwell.

Burr, L. (1988). 'Psychometricity – The Philosophy and Practice'. *Paediatric Interest People*, Spring, 1988, pp. 11–12.

Butler, D. (1980). *Babies Need Books.* Harmondsworth: Penguin.

Calkins, L. M. (1983). *Lessons from a Child on the Teaching and Learning of Writing.* London: Heinemann.

Calkins, L. M. (1986). *The Art of Teaching Writing.* London: Heinemann.

Chomsky, C. (1970). 'Reading, Writing and Phonology'. *Harvard Educational Review*, **40**: 287–309.

Clark, M. M. (1979, 2nd ed.). *Reading Difficulties in Schools.* London: Heinemann.

Clay, M. M. (1982). *Observing Young Readers: Selected Papers.* London: Heinemann.

Clay, M. M. (1985, 3rd ed.). *The Early Detection of Reading Difficulties.* London: Macmillan.

Clay, M. (1975). *What Did I Write?* London: Heinemann.

Cox, C. B. (1988). *English for Ages 5–11.* London: HMSO.

Cox, C. B. (1989). *English for Ages 5–16.* London: HMSO.

Craft, M., Raynor, J. and Cohen, L. (1980, 3rd ed.). *Linking Home and School.* London: Harper & Row.

Cratty, B. J. (1974). *Remedial Motor Activity for Children.* Philadelphia: Lea & Fabinger.

Cripps, C. and Cox, R. (1987). 'Joining the abc'. In *Support for Learning*, vol. 2, no. 4. London: Longman.

Critchley, M. (1964). *The Dyslexic Child.* London: Heinemann.

Crompton, R. (ed.) (1989). *Computers and the Primary Classroom.* Lewes: Falmer.

Cruikshank, W. M. and Hallam, D. P. (1973). *Psycho-educational Foundations of Learning Disabilities.* London: Prentice-Hall.

Doehring, D. G., Trites, R. L., Patel, P. G. and Fiedorowicz, C. A. M. (1981). *Reading Disabilities: The Interaction of Reading, Language and Neuropsychological Deficits.* London: Academic Press.

Doman, G. (1965). *Teach Your Baby to Read.* London: Cape.

Donaldson, M. (1978). *Children's Minds.* London: Collins.

Douglas, J. W. B. (1967). *The Home and the School.* London: Panther.

Edwards, B. (1979). *Drawing on the Right Side of the Brain.* Los Angeles: Tarcher.

Ellis, A. W. (1984). *Reading, Writing and Dyslexia*. London: Erlbaum.

Farnham-Diggory, S., Bruner, J., Cole, M. and Lloyd, B. (eds.) (1984). *Learning Disabilities: The Developing Child*. London: Collins.

Fernald, G. (1943). *Remedial Techniques in Basic School Subjects*. New York: McGraw Hill.

Ferreiro, E. and Teberosky, A. (1983). *Literacy Before Schooling*. London: Heinemann.

Franklin, A. W. and Naidoo, S. (eds.) (1970). *Assessment and Teaching of Dyslexic Children*. London: ICAA.

Frith, U. (1984). 'Specific Spelling Problems'. In Malatesha, R. N. and Whitaker, H. A. (eds.) *Dyslexia: A Global Issue*. The Hague: Martinus Nijhoff.

Frith, U. (1980). 'Unexpected Spelling Problems'. In Frith, U. (ed.) *Cognitive Processes in Spelling*. London: Academic Press.

Frith, U. (1985). 'Beneath the Surface of Developmental Dyslexia'. In Patterson, K. E., Marshall, J. C. and Coltheart, M. (eds.) *Surface Dyslexia*. London: Routledge.

Gardner, H. (1980). *Artful Scribbles*. London: Jill Norman Books.

Gardner, H. (1983). *Frames of Mind*. London: Granada.

Garrett, J. and Dyke, R. (1988). *Microelectronics and Pupils with Special Needs*. Manchester: Manchester University Press.

Gartner, A., Kohler, M. and Riessman, F. (1971). *Children Teach Children: Learning by Teaching*. London: Harper & Row.

Glynn, T. (1985). 'Remedial Reading at Home'. In Topping, K. and Wolfendale, S. (eds.) *Parental Involvement in Children's Reading*. London: Croom Helm.

Goelman, H. *et al.* (1984). *Awakening to Literacy*. London: Heinemann.

Goodenough, S. (ed.) (1989). *Art Ability*. London: Carnegie UK Trust, Russell.

Goodlad, S. (1979) *Learning by Teaching: An Introduction to Tutoring*. London: Community Service Volunteers.

Goodlad, S. and Hirst, B. (1989). *Peer Tutoring: A Guide to Learning by Teaching*. London: Kogan Page.

Gordon, N. and McKinlay, I. (1980) *Helping Clumsy Children*. London: Churchill Livingstone.

Goswami, U. (1988). 'Children's Use of Analogy in Learning to Spell'. *British Journal of Developmental Psychology*, **6**: 21-34.

Graves, D. (1983). *Writing: Teachers and Children at Work*. Exeter: Heinemann.

Graves, M. (1977). *A Highly Structured Tutoring Program for Secondary School Students Seriously Deficient in Reading Skills*. Paper presented at the Annual Meeting of the International Reading Association, Miami, Florida, May 2-6 1977.

Greening, M. and Spenceley, J. (1987). 'Shared Reading: Support for Inexperienced Readers'. *Educational Psychology in Practice*, vol. 3, no. 1, 31-37.

Griffiths, A. and Hamilton, D. (1984). *Parent, Teacher, Child: Working Together in Children's Learning*. London: Methuen.

Gulbenkian Foundation Inquiry (1981). *The Arts in Schools*. Philadelphia.

149

Hannon, P. and Jackson, A. (1987). *The Belfield Reading Project Final Report*. London: National Children's Bureau.

Hansen, G. (1986). *Co-operative vs. Individual Learning: Effects on Vocabulary Retention*. Thesis, Kean College of New Jersey.

Harrison, C. (1980). *Readability in the Classroom*. Cambridge: CUP.

Heath, S. B. (1983). *Ways with Words: Language, Life and Work in Communities and Classroom*. Cambridge: CUP.

Henderson, E. H. (1980). 'Developmental Concepts of Word'. In Henderson, E. H. and Beers, J. W. (eds.) *Developmental and Cognitive Aspects of Learning to Spell: A Reflection of Word Knowledge*. Newark, Delaware: International Reading Association.

Hickey, K. (1977). *Dyslexia: A Language Training Course for Teachers and Learners*. London: Kathleen Hickey Publications.

Hildreth, G. (1936). 'Developmental Sequences in Name Writing'. *Child Development*, vol. 7: 291–303.

Hornsby, B. and Shear, F. (1976). *Alpha to Omega*. London: Heinemann.

Hunter, P. (1989). 'The Writing Process and Word-Processing'. *Microscope Summer Special*. Newman College with MAPE.

Jarman, C. (1981). 'Writing Wrongs'. *Times Educational Supplement*, 11/12/81.

Jorm, A. F. (1983). *The Psychology of Reading and Spelling Disabilities*. London: Routledge.

Kellogg, R. (1969). *Analysing Children's Art*. London: Muller.

Kennedy, M. (1989). 'Controlled Evaluation of the Effects of Peer Tutoring on the Tutors: Are the "Learning by Teaching" Theories Viable?': a paper presented at the Peer Tutoring Conference, London, April 3–5.

Kephart, N. C. (1960). *The Slow Learner in the Classroom*. Ohio: Merrill.

Klein, M. D. (1982). *Pre-Writing Skills*. Arizona: Communication Skill Builders.

Klein, M. D. (1987). *Pre-Scissor Skills*. Arizona: Therapy Skill Builders.

Laszlo, J. I. and Bairstow, P. J. (1985). *Perceptual Motor Behaviour Development Assessment and Therapy*. London: Holt, Reinhart & Winston.

Levitt, S. (ed.) (1984). *Pediatric Development Therapy*. Oxford: Blackwell.

Liberman, I. Y., Shankweiler, D., Liberman, A., Fowler, C. and Fisher, F. W. (1977). 'Phonetic Segmentation and Recoding in the Beginning Reader'. In Reber, A. S. and Scarbrough, D. L. *Towards a Psychology of Reading*. Hillsdale, NJ: Erlbaum.

Mann, V. A., Tobin, P. and Wilson, R. (1987). 'Measuring Phonological Awareness through the Invented Spellings of Kindergarten Children'. *Merrill-Palmer Quarterly*, vol. 33, no. 3: 365–391.

Martin, N. (1983). *Mostly about Writing: Selected Essays*. London: Heinemann.

Martin, T. (1989). *The Strugglers*. Milton Keynes: Open University.

Meek, M. (1982). *Learning to Read*. London: Bodley Head.

Miles, E. (1989). *The Bangor Dyslexia System*. London: Whurr.

Miles, T. R. and Miles, E. (1983). *Help for Dyslexic Children*. London: Methuen.

Morgan, R. (1986). *Helping Children Read*. London: Methuen.

150

Morris, P. E. and Hampson, P. J. (1983). *Imagery and Consciousness*. London: Academic Press.

Naidoo, S. (1972). *Specific Dyslexia*. London: Pitman.

Nash-Wortham, M. (1987). 'The Clumsy, Poorly Co-ordinated Child with Associated Speech, Reading and Writing Difficulties'. *Support for Learning', vol.* 2, 4: 36–40.

National Writing Project (1989). *Responding to and Assessing Writing*. Walton-on-Thames: Nelson.

Newson, J. and Newson, E. (1977). *Perspectives on School at Seven Years Old*. London: Allen & Unwin.

Osguthorpe, R. T. and Scruggs, T. (1986). 'Special Education Students as Tutors: A Review and Analysis'. *Remedial and Special Education*, vol. 7(4): 15–26.

Pavlidis, G. T. and Miles, T. R. (1981). *Dyslexia Research and its Application to Education*. Chichester: Wiley.

Pavlidis, G. T. and Fisher, D. E. (eds.) (1986). *Dyslexia: Its Neuropsychology and Treatment*. Chichester: Wiley.

Payton, S. (1984). *Developing Awareness of Print: A Child's First Steps Towards Literacy*. Birmingham: Educational Review No. 2, University of Birmingham.

Perry, L. and Swapp, J. (eds.) (1987). *Gnosis No. 10: Assessment*. London: ILEA.

Peters, M. L. (1985, revised ed.) *Spelling Taught or Caught?* London: Routledge.

Peters, M. L. and Cripps, C. (1978). *Catchwords: Ideas for Teaching Spelling*. London: Harcourt Brace Jovanovich.

Pinsent, P. A. (ed.) (1989). *Spotlight on Spelling*. Bicester: AB Academic Publishers.

Plowden Report (1967). *Children and Their Primary Schools*. London: HMSO.

Pumfrey, P. D. (1985). *Reading: Tests and Assessment Techniques* 2nd ed. London: Hodder & Stoughton.

Quin, V. and MacAuslan, A. (1981). *Reading and Spelling Difficulties: A Medical Approach*. London: Hodder & Stoughton.

Read, C. (1986). *Children's Creative Spelling*. London: Routledge.

Read, H. (1958). *Education Through Art*. London: Faber.

Reading 360 (1984). London: Ginn.

Richmond, J., Joyner, J. *et al.* (eds.) (1988). *The English Curriculum: Writing*. London: ILEA (NATE).

Roberts, K. (1980). 'Schools, Parents and Social Class'. In Craft *et al.*, op.cit.

Rubens, M. and Newland, M. (1989). *A Tool for Learning: Some Functions of Art in Primary Education*. Ipswich: Direct Experience & Gulbenkian Foundation.

Russell, J. P. (1988). *Graded Activities for Children with Motor Difficulties*. Cambridge: Cambridge University Press.

Rye, J. (1982). *Cloze Procedure and the Teaching of Reading*. London: Heinemann.

Southgate, V. *et al.* (1981). *Extending Beginning Reading*. London: Heinemann.

Schonnell, F. J. (1942). *Backwardness in the Basic Subjects*. London: Oliver and Boyd.

Smith, F. (1984). *Joining the Literacy Club*. Reading: Centre for the Teaching of Reading, Reading University, in conjunction with Abel Press, Victoria B.C.

Snowling, M. J. (1987). *Dyslexia: A Cognitive Developmental Perspective*. Oxford: Blackwell.

Springer, S. P. and Deutsch, G. (1981). *Left Brain, Right Brain*. New York: Freeman.

Stollard, J. (1988). 'Children with Fine Motor Difficulties – Developing Handwriting'. *Gnosis*, 12: 12–19.

Stubbs, M. (1980). *Language and Literacy: The Sociolinguistics of Reading and Writing*. London: Routledge.

Tansley, A. E. (1980). *Motor Education*. Leeds: Arnold Wheaton.

Tansley, A. E. (1967). *Reading and Remedial Reading*. London: Routledge.

Taylor Report (1977). *A New Partnership for Our Schools*. London: HMSO.

Temple, C. A., Nathan, R. G. and Burris, N. A. (1988, 2nd ed.). *The Beginnings of Writing*. Boston: Allyn & Bacon.

Thelen, H. A. (1969). 'Tutoring by Students'. *The School Review*, 77(33): 229–244.

Tizard, B. and Hughes, M. (1984). *Young Children Learning*. London: Collins.

Tizard, J. and Hewison, J. (1980). 'Parental Involvement and Reading Attainment'. *British Journal of Educational Psychology*, vol. 50: 209–215.

Tizard, J., Schofield, W. N. and Hewison, J. (1982). 'Collaboration between Teachers and Parents in Assisting Children's Reading'. *British Journal of Educational Psychology*, vol. 52: 1–15.

Topping, K. (1988). *Paired Reading Training Pack* (3rd ed.). Huddersfield: Kirklees Psychological Service.

Topping, K. (1986). *Parents as Educators: Training Parents to Teach Their Children*. London: Croom Helm.

Topping, K. (1987). 'Peer Tutored Paired Reading: Outcome Data from 10 Projects'. *Educational Psychology*, vol. 7, no. 2: 33–144.

Topping, K. (1988). *Peer Tutoring Handbook: Promoting Co-operative Learning*. London: Croom Helm.

Topping, K. and Wolfendale, S. (1985). *Parental Involvement in Children's Reading*. London: Croom Helm.

Van Sommers, P. (1984). *Drawing and Cognition*. Cambridge: Cambridge University Press.

Vincent, D. *et al.* (1983). *A Review of Reading Tests*. Windsor: NFER-Nelson.

Warnock Report (1978). *Special Educational Needs*. London: HMSO.

Wells, G. (1986). *The Meaning Makers*. London: Hodder & Stoughton.

Widlake, P. (ed.) (1989). *Special Children Handbook*. London: Hutchinson.

Wilkinson, A. *et al.* (1980). *Assessing Language Development*. Oxford: Oxford University Press.

Winter, S. (1988). 'Paired Reading: A Study of Process and Outcome'. *Educational Psychology*, vol. 8, no. 3: 135–151.

Winter, S. (1986). 'Peers as Paired Reading Tutors'. *British Journal of Special Education*, vol. 13, no. 2.

Wright, B. (1960). 'Should Children Teach?'. *Elementary School Journal*, **60**: 353–369.

Young, M. and McGeeney, P. (1968). *Learning Begins at Home*. London: Routledge.

Young, P. and Tyre, C. (1983). *Dyslexia or Illiteracy?: Realising the Right to Read*. Milton Keynes: Open University.

Young, P. and Tyre, C. (1985). *Teach Your Child to Read*. London: Collins.

Index of Subjects

Index of Authors